KU-548-469

Education and personal relationships

A Philosophical Study

Education and personal relationships

A Philosophical Study R. S. Downie
Eileen M. Loudfoot
Elizabeth Telfer

Methuen & Co Ltd 11 New Fetter Lane
London EC4

59854

First published 1974 by Methuen & Co Ltd
11 New Fetter Lane, London EC4P 4EE
© *1974 R. S. Downie, Eileen M. Loudfoot*
and Elizabeth Telfer
Printed in Great Britain by
Richard Clay (The Chaucer Press) Ltd
Bungay, Suffolk

ISBN 0 416 76160 7 (hardbound)
ISBN 0 416 76210 7 (paperback)

Distributed in the USA by
Harper & Row Publishers Inc.
Barnes and Noble Import Division

Contents

Preface

The philosophy of education is in a sense a very old subject in that all the major philosophers from Plato onwards have contributed to it. But it has recently had something of a renaissance. One reason for this is that contemporary philosophers have been broadening their horizons during the past decade and are now willing to apply to the concepts of education the rigorous and careful argumentation which previously they reserved for the theory of knowledge and moral philosophy. A second reason is that educationists are now more willing to listen to philosophers than they were some time ago and to find interest and profit in philosophical discussion. Certainly, our own experience of reading papers to societies concerned with the philosophy of education suggests that there can be a helpful exchange of ideas between philosophers and educationists. This book is mainly the outcome of many such occasions when we have been stimulated by the arguments of those who, while they may not have been trained as philosophers, nevertheless relish the discussion of philosophical problems. We are grateful for having been forced to clarify and develop the views which we now express in this book.

In Chapters One and Two we are concerned with what it is to be a teacher and what it is to be educated, and in Chapters Three and Four we consider what kinds of justification can be given for the pursuit of education so conceived. Our view is that it makes for clearer discussion of what should be done in schools, or of how the government should spend its money, or of what choices individual pupils ought to make, if the term 'education' is not stretched in all directions to include every worthwhile activity which goes on in educational institutions, but rather is given a reasonably definite – even a restricted – sense. In Chapters Five and Six we examine topics such as the nature of personal and impersonal relationships, and concepts such as friendship and paternalism, and try to show the relevance of these ideas to the many possible relationships which are to be found in an educational context. In our postscript we consider the typical objections which we have encountered in discussions with students and teachers. The aim of our discussion is principally to contribute to the theoretical understanding of these complex ideas, but we hope that it will also have a bearing on important practical problems facing those (and they include almost everyone) with some sort of stake in education.

Department of Moral Philosophy
University of Glasgow.

Chapter One

Introduction: the concept of a teacher

People teach each other many things in the course of their everyday lives. There is a distinction, however, between *teaching*, in the sense of simply explaining something to someone, and *being a teacher*, in the sense which designates one kind of occupation. (The same holds, *mutatis mutandis*, of being a pupil.) It is the latter sense on which we shall concentrate here. What then is the general nature of the concept of a teacher so understood?

1 Role-jobs, skill-jobs and aim-jobs

As a start in answering this question we shall introduce a way of describing or classifying occupations which brings out some important conceptual features. Occupations can be described or classified from three different points of view, or in terms of three different sets of concepts: as role-jobs, skill-jobs and aim-jobs. Let us begin the analysis of these distinctions by considering the difference between role-jobs and skill-jobs, or role-job-descriptions and skill-job-descriptions.[1]

The job of Income Tax Inspector or Lord Mayor is a role-job, 'role' here being defined in terms of a set of rights and duties. In contrast, the job of musician is defined in terms of a skill, or set of

[1] See Eileen M. Loudfoot, 'The Concept of Social Role', *Philosophy of the Social Sciences*, 1972.

skills – to be a musician one logically must have certain skills. This is not to say that certain skills are not in fact required for the job of Lord Mayor or Income Tax Inspector to be carried out successfully, but it is to say that an adequate definition of the jobs need contain no reference to these skills. On the other hand, a reference to the relevant skills is logically required for an adequate definition of the jobs of musician or philosopher; we can claim that the statement 'X is a musician/philosopher' is analytically connected with the statement 'X is skilled at music/philosophy'. Thus, if someone claims to be a musician but is clearly unskilled, we can truly say 'He's no musician', meaning that he does not have the skill necessary for membership of the class of musicians. If, however, an Income Tax Inspector is incompetent, or a Lord Mayor persistently makes mistakes, we cannot truly say 'He's no Income Tax Inspector', or 'He's no Lord Mayor'. If we used the form of words we would in fact mean 'He is a bad Income Tax Inspector', or 'He is no good as a Lord Mayor'. In general, the distinction between role-jobs and skill-jobs can be stated as follows: the connexion between a skill-job and the possession of an ability is a logical one, whereas the connexion between a role-job and the possession of an ability is a pragmatic one – a person may in practice need certain skills in order to acquire a role-job or to perform it well, but possessing the skills is not part of the definition of the job.

One reason why it is easy to confuse role-jobs and skill-jobs is that, in certain contexts, skill-jobs become institutionalized. Thus, while 'philosopher' is a skill-job, 'professor of philosophy' is a role-job. That is to say, there are certain institutional rights and duties which enter into the definition of the latter in addition to the skills which are logically necessary to being a philosopher *simpliciter*. Similarly, although 'musician' is a skill-job, 'leader of the band' is a role-job as well.

Let us turn to aim-jobs. It would seem to be the case that a number of occupations are defined in terms of some end or aim. For example, the job of 'farmer' can be said to be an aim-job, in that to be a farmer is to aim at cultivation, milk or beef production or whatever. Similarly, the job of 'forester' is defined in terms of an aim, and also the job of 'gamekeeper'. It is not necessary that the aim be always attained, and obviously skill in the choosing and implementing of means will have a bearing here, but before a person can be described as a farmer, a forester, a gamekeeper, etc. he must at least see himself as aiming at a certain end. We would call a man a *bad* farmer if he chose the wrong means to an end, or was unskilful at implementing the means, but if he is not pursuing the end at all then he is not a farmer. The same would hold for all who profess occupations which are aim-jobs. In general, then, to say that A, B or C is an aim-job, is to say that there exists some purpose, aim or end which is logically connected with job A, B or C. It is to say that unless a person has the aim in question, he cannot be counted as a member of the class of those who have jobs A, B or C.

We have previously said that a role-job, although defined in terms of a set of rights and duties, may in fact require on the part of its occupant certain skills in order that the role be enacted satisfactorily. Now it is also the case that a role-job may be directed towards a certain end, but once again the important point is that the role-occupant, e.g. the Lord Mayor or Income Tax Inspector, who has little success in attaining the end is not 'not a role-occupant' or 'not a Lord Mayor at all'. He may be a *bad* Lord Mayor if he never bothers about working out a viable policy, but he is not 'not a Lord Mayor at all', for the job of Lord Mayor is not defined in terms of an aim. In the same way, a skill-job may or may not be directed towards an end, but this does not have bearing on its definition. For example, the aim of musicianship might by some be said to be the maintenance of a high level of culture within a community. But the individual musician need have no aim of this sort to be a musician; his concern is properly with the exercise of his skill.

We have tended to speak so far as if there were three types of job, and this is so in the sense that some jobs are to be defined in terms of one or other of the three categories of role, aim or skill. And it is so irrespective of the fact that many jobs, while they may be defined in one of the three ways, clearly involve the other categories also. In the case of some jobs, however, it is not so obvious that they are to be defined in one category rather than another, and at any rate they certainly involve all three. The job of teacher is perhaps the best example of this. For 'teacher' cannot be defined exclusively by reference to any one of the three categories, but requires to be placed in all three. To bring this out let us consider teaching first in terms of its end or aim. What is the aim of the teacher?

2 'Teacher' as an aim-job

It might be objected immediately that there is no one aim of the teacher; different teachers have different aims and one and the same teacher may have many aims. For example, teachers might be said to aim at teaching history or whatever, at producing good citizens, at earning their own salary. Again, in the course of a day a given teacher might aim at explaining the theory of logarithms, at selling tickets for the school concert and at keeping the noise to a minimum in 2E. The reply to this objection is not to abandon the search for the aim of the teacher but rather to introduce a few distinctions in the concept of an aim as it applies to the job of teacher.

In the first place, a person who happens to be a teacher will have various aims which are not necessarily connected with his occupation, although they are furthered through it. Let us call these his 'personal aims'. For example, he might aim at earning his living, at having good opportunities for badminton or at sublimating his deviant sexual tendencies. These are legitimately regarded as among his aims as a teacher, in that he fulfils them by means of his occupation, but they are not connected with his occupation as such since they might just as easily be satisfied in other occupations. Hence, they can be identified as 'personal aims'. Secondly, a teacher will have various aims or ends which do arise for him *as a result of* his job, but are not *logically* connected with his job. For example, he might aim at encouraging his pupils to take an interest in their personal appearance, or he might aim at drawing out the personality of some retiring pupil, or at having some suspected physical ailment in a pupil investigated by a doctor. Let us call these 'ancillary aims'. Unlike the first kind they are connected with the job of the teacher, in that they arise because the person has the job of teacher, rather than being connected simply with the private interests of the person who happens to be the teacher. But they are not what we might regard as aims which enter into the definition of the teacher. A good teacher will have a general interest in his pupils and will certainly pursue many such aims, but they are ancillary to his aims *qua* teacher; they remove impediments from or add incentives to the pupil's pursuit of education, but they are not themselves of the essence of education. Indeed, although the teacher ought always himself to be on the lookout for such impediments or incentives there may well be an ancillary service in schools concerned with at least some of these medical or psychological matters.

Thirdly, and most importantly, there is what we shall call the 'intrinsic aim' of the teacher, which logically must be entertained by the teacher *qua* teacher. We shall state here quite baldly what we shall elaborate in subsequent chapters, that the intrinsic aim of the teacher is education. To attempt to say what education, the intrinsic aim of the teacher, consists in is to provide an account of the descriptive meaning of 'education', and this we attempt to do. By 'education' we mean 'the cultivation of the mind, or theoretical reason, and the transmission of culture' and we shall go on in Chapter Two to say what this amounts to. This narrow, descriptive account of education will rule out as part of education various activities which go on in schools, so a question might be raised as to the justification for our stipulation. The justification is that a number of activities have in common that they exercise the mind or theoretical reason and it is convenient to use the term 'education' as a way of referring to these activities. The term 'education' is, of course, used in other ways, but our view is that clarity is a casualty of the attempt to broaden the concept of education so that every new activity of a school is part of 'education', and that the alternatives for social policy and individual choice can be considered more clearly if, for example, we *contrast* the benefits to society of spending money on education with those of spending it on outdoor adventure courses, rather than say that outdoor adventure courses are 'part of education'.

It is possible, however, to aim at further ends to be attained through education, such as fitting pupils for employment, or creating the conditions for their future happiness, or producing useful citizens. These aims, insofar as they are attained *through* education, we shall call, fourthly, the 'extrinsic aims' of the teacher. To ask about the extrinsic aim of the teacher is to ask what he might hope to achieve not so much *in* his teaching but *as a result of* his teaching, meaning by that the non-educational consequences of it. We shall provide some suggestions on this topic in Chapter Four.

It should be noted, to avoid confusion, that what we have been contrasting as the intrinsic and extrinsic aims of the *teacher* can also be expressed in terms of the intrinsic and extrinsic aims of *education*. Using the term 'education' we might make the desired contrast by opposing aims *in* education (what education consists of) with aims *for* education (what use is made of education). We shall adopt the terminology of 'education' for reasons of convenience in Chapters Two to Four, but speak of the 'teacher' in Chapters Five and Six when we deal with roles and personal relationships. Let us in the meantime return to the classification of the aims of the teacher.

There are, fifthly, aims which in some ways resemble the intrinsic aims of the teacher in that they are educational aims, but in a sense of the term 'education' rather broader than that we propose to employ. For example, school pupils might learn cookery or flower-arranging, or typing or chess. We shall call this fifth variety 'complementary aims'. The point is that there are important skills, vocational or domestic or for the enrichment of leisure, which people are the better for possessing, and there is a good opportunity to instruct young people in these skills when they are at school; but these skills are not in our strict sense *education*. In Chapter Two we shall try to explain in some detail what we mean by education in the strict sense, but in the meantime we simply note that there are legitimate – indeed, highly desirable – activities in schools which are concerned with education only in the vaguest sense, that in which anything which happens in a school is called 'education'.

We have identified briefly five aims which a teacher may in fact have at any given time, and our point is that only one of these – the intrinsic aim of education – is the aim of the teacher *qua* teacher (although the others are legitimate or desirable aims). Before leaving the topic let us draw attention to one complexity in it. Some subjects taught in schools can fall into several categories depending on how they are taught. Take, for example, what is nowadays called physical education. If this is intended simply to be exercise for the pupils to keep them healthy for their studies, then it is what we are calling an 'ancillary aim'. If it is intended not only to keep the pupils healthy but also to provide them with skills, in sports, say, which will be useful in later life, then it is also a complementary aim. Suppose, however, that it is taught in such a way as to give pupils an understanding of the workings of their bodies and of the ways in which bodily movements can express emotion; then it has become education proper. Finally, suppose that a teacher of physical education proper, one who is pursuing the intrinsic aims we have just described, also aims at enabling his pupils, via physical education, to lead happier lives, to be more useful citizens and so on – then he is entertaining the extrinsic aims of education.

3 Justifications of education

Our account of the logically distinct aims which a teacher may have is partly intended to give us the conceptual apparatus which will enable us to isolate a definite but narrow concept of the teacher and of education. But it is also intended to give us the apparatus to examine possible justifications for the pursuit of education thus narrowly conceived. Before we outline these we should note an ambiguity in the term 'education'. The term can be used either for the process of educating or for the end-result of that process, the state of educatedness. The first sense is employed in sentences like 'Education in this country takes place during childhood'; the second in sentences like 'Education is no substitute for character'. We have therefore the *process* of educating, which is directed towards producing the *state* of educatedness. The teacher whose intrinsic aim is education, or at least making a contribution to someone's education, is aiming at both of these things, but in two different senses: in aiming to make a contribution to his pupils' educatedness, as the future goal of his teaching, he is also by definition aiming at a present and continuous goal – that his teaching may be a case of educating.

So far we have spoken as though the aim of educating is some future state of educatedness – a kind of harvest reaped in the future as a return for present endeavour. But this account may mislead, for there is no point in time at which a person can be said to be completely educated, as though he were a house which is said to be completely decorated. This is so for two reasons: firstly, educatedness is a matter of degree and so is not achieved at a given point, though it is true that we often speak of an 'educated person', as if some kind of completion had been attained. In other words, a state of educatedness is something that is gradually acquired all the time, so that a person who is being educated is already acquiring the state as the process continues. Secondly, the content of educatedness – what the educated man knows – is growing and changing all the time because of the development of knowledge and the continuing practice of the arts. It is therefore logically impossible for anyone, however gifted, to complete his education. Education must be a continuing process, and as we shall see in the next chapter the so-called 'educated man' is, among other things, the man who has acquired the capacities and the inclinations to continue the process.

Assuming that it is educatedness that we are basically considering when we raise the question of justification, we shall examine in Chapters Three and Four the sorts of justification which can be offered for pursuing it. It might be objected that surely education as such needs no justification because it is by definition something worthwhile for its own sake. In reply we can admit that people do use the word 'education' to mean 'whatever development or cultivation of a person is worthwhile', thus robbing the word of most of its descriptive meaning. Clearly, on such an approach, the problem of the justification of education logically cannot arise. The question of whether the word 'education' is taken as having a fairly definite descriptive meaning and little evaluative force or as having built-in evaluative force and no definite descriptive meaning is a matter settled by choice for different purposes. For reasons of clarity which we explained in our preface and in the previous section we have decided on the first alternative, and intend to explicate the descriptive meaning which we believe the word commonly possesses. But as a consequence of this decision we are faced with the task of examining the possible justifications of education. It should be noted that our conceptual decision does not rule out the possibility that education is worthwhile in itself, only the possibility that it is so by *definition*, that someone who denies it to be so does not understand the concept. We shall not ignore the important theories which claim that education (educatedness) is its own justification or is just worthwhile in itself and we shall consider them in Chapter Three. But there are also important attempts to justify the pursuit of educatedness in terms of its extrinsic aims (aims for education), and we therefore propose to spend some time in Chapter Four examining them. Whether in terms of its intrinsic or its extrinsic aims the question of the justification of the pursuit of educatedness is an important one: it arises for governments who rightly want to know why they should pay large sums of money for this rather than meet other demands on their resources; it arises for people wondering whether to choose teaching as a career, and it arises for children and their parents wondering whether or not to choose to undertake further education.

We have already said that problems of the same sort arise whether we speak of the aims of the teacher or the aims of education. Our plan is to discuss the intrinsic aim of the teacher and to regard that as education or educatedness descriptively conceived. We shall then discuss the extrinsic aims of the teacher (aims for education, or attempted justifications of education), and complementary and ancillary aims. Some personal aims will be discussed in the different context of personal relationships in education.

4 'Teacher' as a skill-job and a role-job

We have spent some time on the idea of the job of teacher from the point of view of its aims because the conceptual distinctions required are not straightforward. It is easier to introduce the ideas of 'teacher' as a skill-job and 'teacher' as a role-job. A teacher is not merely a person who aims at creating a state of educatedness in others; he is also the possessor of a certain expertise in doing so, lack of which justifies others in saying 'He's no teacher'. To consider what is involved in this expertise is to consider the sense in which 'teacher' is a skill-job. Of course, a teacher requires many skills and it might be thought difficult to make any general remarks about them. It is possible, however, at least to suggest important limitations to the types of skill which a teacher ought to use on his pupils. The nature of these limitations will emerge when we discuss in Chapter Two what educatedness consists in.

The job of the teacher must also be seen as a social role. There is an obvious sense in which this is so: the teacher will be the employee of a local authority, a board of governors or the like, and like any employee will have duties to and rights against his employer. But there are more important reasons, connected with the nature of teaching as such, why teaching must be seen as a role-job, and one which involves far more than the role-relationship with the teacher's employer. We shall develop an account of teaching as a role-job in Chapter Five.

Chapter Two

The aim and the skill
of the teacher

We have argued in our first chapter that the teacher *qua* teacher aims at education (whatever else the individual teacher may also do), or that the education of his pupils is his intrinsic aim. We also argued that, while the term 'education' can be used in a very wide evaluative way such that whatever education is it is necessarily worth pursuing, it can also be used more narrowly and descriptively, in a way which leaves open the question of whether education in this sense is a good thing. In the first two sections of this chapter we propose to add details to this narrow picture of the educated man which it is the intrinsic aim of the teacher to produce, and in the third section we shall make some philosophical (as distinct from pedagogical) points about the nature of the skills which help to produce the educated man.

1 The educated man: knowledge that, *understanding, knowledge* how *and inclinations*

We shall begin by clearing away two possible confusions. When we say 'educated' we are not using the word to mean 'middle-class', as in 'No educated person would speak like that'. Nor are we referring simply to those who have 'been through' particular educational establishments, such as universities, as in the *Who's Who* entries which read 'Educated at . . .'. We do not wish to rule out by definition the possibility of someone's being self-educated. On the contrary, the educated man is distinguishable by what he is and does, not by where he comes from. What, then, are the distinguishing features of the educated man?

We shall argue that the knowledge he possesses has certain characteristics, that he has a certain sort of understanding of that knowledge, and certain inclinations or dispositions with respect to it. In characterizing the knowledge we have found it helpful to adopt the traditional distinctions between knowledge *that*, knowledge *how*, and knowledge *by acquaintance*.[1] These ways of categorizing knowledge are not without their problems and obscurities, and a work devoted to the theory of knowledge might well cast serious doubt on their ultimate validity as distinctions. But for our purposes the distinctions have a heuristic value, for they enable us to bring out important points about the nature of education which are less conveniently discussed in other ways; accordingly, we shall assume the distinctions for purposes of argument. We shall begin by investigating the nature of the knowledge *that* possessed by the educated man and what it is for him to understand that knowledge. We shall then discuss his knowledge *how*, and his inclinations or dispositions with respect to his knowledge *that* and *how*. We shall defer to the second section of the chapter consideration of knowledge *by acquaintance*, which raises different but analogous problems.

By knowledge *that* we mean 'justified true belief',[2] and our problem is that of deciding how to characterize the justified true beliefs of the educated man. We suggest that they are of wide-ranging scope, important, relevant and grounded. It should be noted that we are here making a logical claim; in other words, we are making it necessary in virtue of the meaning we are attaching to the term 'educated' that the knowledge *that* of the educated man has these features. Let us now examine them in more detail.

[1] See D. W. Hamlyn, *The Theory of Knowledge*, pp. 103–6 and references there (London, Macmillan, Modern Introductions to Philosophy, 1970).

[2] For an account of the nature of knowledge, see A. J. Ayer, *The Problems of Knowledge*, ch. I (London, Penguin Books, 1956). See also Hamlyn, op. cit., ch. IV.

The first demand is not problematical: we would not call a man educated who knew everything about history and nothing about science, or everything about literature and nothing about current affairs. The educated man's knowledge must have a wide range, though he may also have specialized knowledge in some spheres. But how can we indicate the different spheres in which the educated man must have knowledge? One possible way is by means of a list of those academic subjects or disciplines in connexion with which it seems most natural to speak of knowledge or of facts as opposed to, say, opinion or doctrine. Such a list would be roughly as follows: history of his own and other cultures, including the history of the arts, of religions, of sciences; geography; the natural sciences; the social sciences; current affairs.

But clearly the educated man cannot know everything in all these disciplines. What we expect him to know are some of the more *important* facts in each sphere. For example, a man is not uneducated if he does not know whether the platypus lays eggs or not; but he is uneducated if he does not know that mammals are the most highly developed branch of the animal kingdom and that they feed their young on milk. Again, a man is not uneducated if he does not know who was the architect of St Peter's in Rome; but he is uneducated if he does not know that in Europe during the fifteenth and sixteenth centuries there was a phenomenon, known as the Renaissance, which sprang from a revived interest in and knowledge of the Greeks and was marked by a new humanism.

But what makes a piece of knowledge important? The examples suggest that an important piece of knowledge is one which has a relatively wide bearing: in other words, one in terms of which other things are explained. The educated man, that is to say, possesses the kinds of knowledge *that* in virtue of which other knowledge *that* can be structured. He cannot however possess only these important or structuring pieces of knowledge, as we shall see shortly when we discuss understanding.

We turn now to the third requirement, that of *relevance* in knowledge *that*. This requirement is rather difficult to define but we can suggest by examples the kind of thing we have in mind. In history we would not call a man educated who knew nothing of Greek and

Roman civilization, but we might do so even if he knew nothing of Indian or Chinese civilization. In biology we would call a man un-educated if he knew nothing of basic human anatomy, but not if he knew nothing of the structure of the crayfish. In social science we would call a man uneducated if he knew nothing of the way his own government is run, but not if he knew nothing of the way the government of Peru is run. These examples all suggest that what is required is that the knowledge *that* should have some bearing on the situation in which the educated man finds himself. The only way to explain why this is held to be so seems to be to say that the educated man is thought of as able to bring an understanding to bear on whatever he comes across, to a degree which the uneducated man cannot. In order to be able to do this he will certainly need relevant knowledge in the sense we have distinguished; we shall say more later about what is involved in his understanding.

But the requirement of relevance raises three problems which must be briefly mentioned. Firstly, it seems to make the content of educatedness partly culture-relative; an educated man in China needs to know different things from an educated man in Britain. This seems an acceptable consequence if we note that there is a large area, even within knowledge *that*, which would be common ground, and that other aspects of educatedness will not be relative at all.

Secondly, it raises a problem about the place of more recondite knowledge in education. Are we saying that study of the govern-ment of Peru is no part of anyone's education (for it certainly goes on in universities)? The answer to this question is threefold. In the first place, some of what goes on in universities (whether done by students or teachers) may be regarded more properly as scholarship or the pursuit of knowledge as such than as education. It does not follow, of course, that it is not worthwhile; but it may require a different kind of justification from education. In the second place, the study may have educational value which is not in terms of the knowledge *that* which is gained: for example, it may be a good way of learning certain methods in political science. In the third place, a piece of knowledge can be relevant in unusual ways; it might be argued that a knowledge of the government of Peru is perfectly relevant, in that it enables its possessor to understand his own government better by providing a comparison and contrast.

The third problem is a possible confusion over this notion of relevance. We are not saying that the relevant knowledge must be *useful* in any practical sense. It may or may not be useful, but the only application which it must have is that it contributes to our *understanding* of our situation. Some may object that some knowledge which is relevant in the sense of 'useful', for example knowledge which would help to alleviate the world's troubles, must be part of people's education. But the 'must' of this thesis is not a logical one, not at least on the conception of the educated man which we are developing, and to build it in to this conception would result, we hold, in a loss of clarity. It is clearer to regard the thesis of the objection as a moral one – 'People ought to be taught, at school and university, knowledge which will help the world' – and then consider how this practically useful knowledge ought to be evaluated against education as we conceive it, if the question arises of the amount of time or money to be spent on each. Sometimes, of course, practically useful knowledge, because of its cognitive content, can be made part of education in our sense, and then there is no practical problem although the two remain theoretically distinct.

The fourth feature possessed by the knowledge *that* of the educated person is that it is *grounded*. Now it may be objected at once that this is part of the very definition of knowledge: knowledge is not merely true belief, but *justified* true belief. But we can distinguish the type of grounding which entitles us to speak of knowledge from that which entitles us to speak of educatedness. The type of grounding which entitles us to speak of knowledge in the educational context concerns partly the usual matters relevant to knowledge, such as evidence and coherence, and partly matters specific to the educational context such as the authority of the teacher's role (teachers are supposed to get things right and to choose textbooks which do so). But simply to say 'Teacher told me', or 'The book said so', though it may be enough in the context of education to enable us to speak of knowledge, is not sufficient for educatedness. The educated person must have some idea of the ways in which the teacher or the book knew – not necessarily in that particular case, but in that kind of case. In other words, the type of grounding which entitles us to speak of educatedness involves additional factors such as a grasp of the methods relevant in these spheres, the types of evidence available in each, the role of observation and of experiment, the ways in which evidence is assessed, the criteria for proof and for a supported hypothesis, and so on. Grounding of the kind required for educatedness cannot be sharply distinguished from the next condition we require the educated man to satisfy – that he should understand his knowledge.

We add this condition because a man might have knowledge *that* with the four features we have discussed and yet not fully *understand* what he knows, and understanding is clearly a feature of the educated man. For example, a person is not educated if he knows that Henry VIII dissolved the monasteries in the 1530s, or that many British birds migrate in winter, but does not understand these items of his knowledge. The understanding required is of several different kinds. Firstly, he must understand the concepts, such as 'dissolved' in this particular sense, used in the propositions expressing his knowledge. Secondly, he must understand *why* what he knows is the case or was the case. Understanding why may take various different forms, depending on the type of knowledge in question: thus understanding why Henry VIII dissolved the monasteries involves reference to his aims and intentions and to the political situation at the time, understanding why birds migrate involves reference to the function which migration serves in the species, understanding why ice floats involves reference to physical laws. (Note that the distinction between understanding the concepts making up one's knowledge and understanding why is often not a sharp one: a word such as 'migration' is a 'theory-loaded' word,[1] carrying with it not merely information about birds flying south, but implications as to the kind of explanation which applies.) Thirdly, the educated man must understand what he knows in the sense of being able to see some of the implications of it, something of what it 'amounts to': for example, to understand one's knowledge that the monasteries were dissolved requires some idea of the effects the dissolution had.

[1] Compare Gilbert Ryle, *The Concept of Mind*, p. 142 (London, Hutchinson's University Library, 1949).

It will now be clear why we said earlier that the educated man cannot possess only important pieces of knowledge: if this were the case he would not understand his knowledge, since he would not realize what it amounted to in more detailed terms.

It is important not to pitch too high the requirement that the educated man must have understanding. He need not understand completely why everything he knows is the case; after all, in some cases the reason why may not be known to anyone. Nor need he understand all the implications of what he knows – if indeed that were possible; but simply be aware of some of the more detailed applications and consequences of the facts as he has them.

It will be seen that understanding a piece of knowledge *that* involves a connexion with other pieces of knowledge *that*, both in understanding why and in understanding implications. But to understand something is not simply to know something else; it is to grasp connexions between various pieces of knowledge, to be able to fit one's knowledge into a framework. We might express this point another way by saying that the educated man's knowledge is structured. It might be objected that using this notion assimilates the requirement of understanding to the requirement of importance in knowledge *that*, where we also spoke of structure. But this is not the case: important knowledge is by definition structur*ing*, but it is not structur*ed* unless its possessor has built it into his house of knowledge, as it were, by understanding why it is so and what it implies.

To have knowledge *that* which is of wide-ranging scope, important, relevant and grounded, and to have understanding of that knowledge, is still not sufficient for educatedness; the educated man must know how to do history, science and so on. It might be objected that this knowledge *how* is really only a species of the understanding *why* which we have just discussed. For example, knowing how to do history might be said to be a matter of understanding why the historian gives special weight to eye-witness accounts, why he ignores the evidence of obviously biased sources, etc. The reply to this objection is that, while it is true that the educated person will indeed understand why the historian does these things, he will also have a knowledge of how to do history which cannot be reduced to any series of statements; he will have developed, at least to a minimum extent, the historian's sense which would enable him to judge whether a suggested new procedure was a reasonable historical procedure or not, or to suggest novel ways of tackling an unusual historical problem; in short, he can do history himself, at least to some degree.

We might compare 'knowing how' in this case to such capacities as 'knowing how to handle a committee'. Doubtless here too there are pieces of knowledge *that* involved: for example, knowing that long speeches bore and annoy committee members. But knowing how to handle a committee does not simply amount to knowing such facts.

It is true that neither knowing how to handle a committee nor knowing how to do history are like some of the paradigm cases of knowing *how*, such as riding a bicycle; for one thing, they incorporate no physical skills. It may even be the case that it is possible after all to express these knowings *how* in terms of some extremely general knowledge *that*. But for our purposes the knowledge to which we have referred as knowing how to do history is sufficiently different in kind from knowing that William the Conqueror invaded Britain in 1066 to warrant the separate categorization.

This kind of knowledge *how*, the grasping of a particular form of thinking and learning,[1] is sometimes spoken of by educators as though it were more important than the knowledge *that* which is gained by it: they say things like 'What is important is not knowing things, but knowing how to find out'. They would of course admit that we need some knowledge *that*, as a means to acquiring the knowledge *how*, but they would regard the knowledge *that* as playing a subsidiary part. But this view seems to us to fail to do justice to the force of the 'knowledge *that*' condition of educatedness. In the first place, the amount of knowledge *that* which would be sufficient to demonstrate methods in a field is far too small to tally with the scope of knowledge which the educated man is expected to have: we might teach someone zoological methods by studying one

[1] For an account of different forms of thought, see P. H. Hirst and R. S. Peters, *The Logic of Education*, pp. 62–6 (London, Routledge and Kegan Paul, The Students Library of Education, 1970).

creature in enormous detail, but he would scarcely be educated if he knew everything about the hamster and nothing about any other creature. Secondly, the pieces of knowledge *that* which a person learnt in learning a form of thinking might be entirely trivial: the details of the Athenian tribute lists furnish a superb example of how history can be learnt from inscriptions, but not of pieces of central historical knowledge. We have therefore two independent criteria for educatedness in these spheres: the possession of knowledge *that* and the possession of knowledge *how*.

We said earlier that whereas pupils might reasonably be said to *know* many things even where their only justification was an appeal to an authority, a person could be said to be *educated* only if he understood how that authority might itself be justified by means of the methods of the study concerned. In other words, to be educated he must learn not only science (for example) but also how to do science. But so far we have not suggested that the educated person is by definition committed to *doing* science, as distinct from learning science and learning how to do science. There is a model of education, however, in terms of 'initiation into worthwhile activities', which does suggest that being educated is precisely being introduced to doing science, doing history and so on.[1] And current educational practice certainly includes the pursuit of what can only be called scientific, historical and sociological research by school-children; in other words, they are beginning to do what a 'real' historian, scientist or sociologist does. Of course, this may be simply as a means to learning *that* ('They'll remember better if they find out for themselves') or to learning *how* ('This will help them to understand what a scientist does') but it need not be so conceived, and presumably is not by the 'initiation' model.

The 'initiation into worthwhile activities' model is problematic in various ways. For one thing, it construes the end of education, or educatedness, as an activity rather than a state. On this view, the educated person seems to be one who *does* certain things, and this is difficult because it seems possible to construe someone as educated even if circumstances force him to do things quite uncharacteristic

[1] See R. S. Peters, *Ethics and Education*, passim, especially ch. II (London, Allen and Unwin, 1966).

of the educated man. But the points stressed by the initiation model can perhaps be put in a weaker and more plausible form, if we say that the educated man has acquired not merely certain intellectual *capacities* which are constituted by his knowledge *that* and his knowledge *how* but also certain *inclinations*, which will lead him to act in certain ways other things being equal. Let us now investigate these inclinations.

The first inclination possessed by the educated man is that of wanting to *apply* his knowledge to the situations in which he finds himself. It might be said that we are here introducing a *moral* thesis of the kind we earlier rejected, about what the educated man ought to do with his knowledge. In reply we can say that the application of knowledge need not be practical, in the sense that the knowledge is used to reach some practical end, such as alleviating distress or making money. Knowledge is being applied just as much if it enables its possessor to understand things. Our demand that the knowledge be applied, then, is a *conceptual* one: that the educated person is one who is not merely *equipped* to understand his world (this is the requirement of relevance) but is also inclined to *use* his knowledge in understanding it. It might be further objected that while our claim that the educated man is inclined to apply his knowledge is indeed a conceptual one, the necessity derives from the concept 'knowledge' rather than the concept 'educated', since to know something is to be disposed to react in various particular ways if appropriate situations arise. But what would be enough for saying simply that a person knows may not be enough for saying that a person has the inclinations to apply his knowledge in the way required for educatedness. Thus, a person who reacts appropriately in a situation in which he is asked 'What does hot air do?' may be said to know that hot air rises. But he is not an educated person unless he has the inclination to apply this knowledge to, let us say, his domestic situation, and thus understand why cakes cook faster at the top of the oven – and it is this kind of desire to apply his knowledge which characterizes the educated person.

This inclination to apply knowledge may be manifested in two different forms. In some straightforward or simple situations – for example, those of a domestic kind, as outlined above – the educated man will automatically apply his knowledge; it is 'second nature' to him, he cannot help doing it. Indeed, this may amount to no more than saying that he understands what he knows in the sense of understanding the implications of it. But not all situations or phenomena are as easily understood, and in the more difficult cases the inclination to apply knowledge will be manifested by the educated man in his making a point of applying what he knows in an effort to reach understanding. Of course, the inclination to apply knowledge in this second way may not always be the strongest inclination in the educated man; the inclination may be overcome by other desires. But a person would not be educated if he never made a point of applying his knowledge in difficult or less obvious cases.

The second inclination possessed by the educated man is the inclination to be *critical*, or at least to test things for himself. Of course, in the case of a generally agreed piece of knowledge there seems no reason why the educated man should be required to test this for himself: indeed, it might be considered a mark of the educated man to recognize when to accept such things. But in the case of an assertion which seems unplausible, or the alleged evidence for which seems inadequate, the educated man will have the inclination to be critical. Again, this inclination may be manifested in two different forms. Firstly, if the faults are obvious the educated man will not be able to stop himself from thinking 'That's insufficient evidence' or 'That's not a random sample' or whatever. If, however, the faults are less obvious, or if the alleged assertion ties in with his vested interests, critical thought will not be automatic but must be voluntarily undertaken; and it is in this second kind of situation that the critical inclination of the educated man is most clearly to be seen.

The strength of this critical inclination must not be exaggerated. For while it seems plausible to say that the educated man must owe allegiance to some kind of standards in thinking, or that a man is not educated unless he is eager to avoid error, this eagerness, like the inclination to apply knowledge, cannot be considered to be by definition the strongest desire in the educated man. In certain circumstances pressures might be sufficient to overwhelm it, and lead him to deceive either himself or others. As an example of the former kind of deception, consider the scientist who asserts a thesis on insufficient evidence, pretending to himself it is sufficient; as an example of the latter, the scientist who consciously fakes his evidence. In neither case would we say that the scientist shows he is not educated after all, in the way we would if it became clear that the scientist genuinely did not understand what he was doing in his work.

We have spoken in terms of 'the avoidance of error', rather than 'the pursuit of truth', quite deliberately; for the latter phrase is ambiguous and covers both the inclination to criticize what is presented and the inclination to find out what is new. The latter inclination, however, is opposed not to error but to ignorance; we may call it, in the third place, *curiosity* or thirst for knowledge. An enormous range of inclinations is included here: the urge to try to explain puzzling phenomena encountered in the course of doing other things, the urge to read books from which more facts can be learnt, the urge to add to the store of the world's knowledge oneself. Moreover, all these urges might manifest either a spontaneous love of discovery, or a more reasoned attitude of respect towards it and acknowledgement of its importance – either the feeling that I want to find out, or that I ought to (or of course a combination of these). It seems clear that teachers would normally aim at producing this range of inclinations in some degree, and would think their work had failed in some measure if an erstwhile pupil was completely indifferent to finding things out. We shall stipulate therefore that the educated man must have some measure of curiosity, though perhaps not the degree necessary to prompt a person into taking up 'research' and though, as in the case of the critical disposition, other factors may prevent the exercise of the curiosity.

We can sum up this discussion by saying that the educated man possesses knowledge *that* which is wide-ranging, important, relevant and grounded, that he *understands* what he knows and also knows *how* to think in these spheres; and educatedness includes also the possession of three inclinations which we can describe as dispositions to apply knowledge, to be critical and to be curious.

2 *The educated man (continued): knowledge by acquaintance, appreciation of values and creativity*

So far we have concentrated on those aspects of educatedness which are concerned most closely with knowledge *that* and to a lesser extent with knowledge *how*. But of course there are many aspects of education which do not fall under what we have said: for example, the appreciation of the arts. We have of course allowed for the straightforward historical aspects of the arts already, but everyone would agree that knowing when Michelangelo lived, what he painted and who commissioned it are not the most important things to know about him. What is missing can best be described as knowledge by *acquaintance*: the educated man not only knows *about* works of art, he knows some of them as individual things.

The conceptual requirements for the educated man's knowledge by acquaintance of works of art are analogous to those governing his knowledge *that*. Firstly, it must be *wide-ranging*, with some acquaintance of different art-forms and of different periods and styles. Secondly, it must include some of the *important* works of art. This means, on the one hand, those works in terms of which others tend to be judged or can be understood; this requirement corresponds to the requirement of importance for knowledge *that*. But 'importance' here also means that some of those works of art thought to be especially fine of their kind must be known by acquaintance by the educated man.

The third requirement is that of *relevance*. As before, the knowledge required for education seems to be culture-relative; a man is considered uneducated in this country if he knows no Shakespeare plays, but not if he knows no Japanese Noh plays. But this demand for relevance in works of art is still ambiguous; is it to be taken to mean 'relevance to our art', or 'relevance to our life in general'? Some would say that, to be worthwhile at all, art (and presumably *a fortiori* art in education) must be relevant to life. But it is not clear how strictly this is to be taken. Music, for example, is scarcely relevant to our lives in any straightforward sense, but people do not argue that it is therefore not a worthwhile art-form. Within other art-forms it would be hard to find a work of art that was *not* relevant to life, at least in the sense of affecting our perceptions of it: knowing an abstract painting by Mondrian or Ben Nicolson can make one aware of pattern in everyday things unnoticed before. And very many works of art are relevant in the stronger sense that they deal with human character and emotions – which are either unchanging or, where changed, illuminating by contrast. Nor need works of art be, or be 'made', topical in order to be relevant in this sense: *Othello* is more relevant regarded as a play about jealousy, passion, stupidity and wickedness than as a play about 'the colour problem'.

But of course it might be insisted (as by Plato in the *Republic*) that art in education be relevant in the sense of being useful, either morally or as a source of knowledge.[1] We shall not here argue against this view but simply take it as axiomatic that art has some kind of intrinsic value or importance, and that this is why the educator aims at enlarging people's acquaintance with it. Not that the proponent of the Platonic view need deny this. He may feel that in bringing works of art before people one can, and perhaps should, serve two purposes at once, moral or intellectual at the same time as aesthetic. But even this attitude is likely to distort the point of art, and lead people to look at it for what they can 'get out of it'.

We suggest, then, that the relevance in question is relevance to our cultural heritage. In so doing, we are espousing the view that art is an activity which creates a world of its own which has an importance not derived from its reflection of the world at large. Of course, these considerations do not by themselves show that a teacher is mistaken in choosing to 'do' a modern play about jealousy – or the colour problem – rather than *Othello*. He might feel that given the particular pupils in question the modern play would more readily supply *other* features required for educated knowledge of a work of art, precisely because it was relevant to life in a fairly crude and obvious sense. For example his pupils might find it easier than *Othello* to appraise and to understand – the two remaining requirements governing the knowledge by acquaintance of the educated man.

We expect that the educated man should know how to, and

[1] Plato, *Republic*, 376E–403C. See also 595A–608B.

should in fact, *appraise* works of art, and that his appraisals should be grounded. Knowledge *by acquaintance* cannot logically itself be grounded, since acquaintance is its own warrant, but grounding is still relevant for another purpose – for judgments of *value*. This requirement of grounded appraisal however is complex. What do we mean by the 'appraisal' of a work of art?

The idea of appraisal involves more than the mere expression of a view, preference or opinion. Thus the person who says 'This painting just appeals to me' is not appraising the work of art; rather he is inarticulately reporting on an instinctive psychological or emotional reaction to it. Nor does appraisal consist simply in expressing a liking for a work of art, even although the statement 'I like it' is accompanied by reasons. For a statement about a work of art to be an appraisal, it is necessary for the person making the statement to have at least some idea of whether, quite apart from liking, it is of good quality as art. And the educated man will be able to make such statements. He will not only be able to say why he likes a work of art, but will also have some idea of whether what he likes is good.

But to put it this way makes it sound a more objective matter than perhaps it is. To know how to judge a painting, say, involves a mixture of objective ways of reasoning with subjective commitments. Objectively speaking there are features which are generally thought of as relevant to the assessment of a picture, and a person who spoke of it with no reference to any of these would not be understood: for example, balance and proportion, richness or subtlety of colour, a sense of light and of depth and so on. But the individual must (logically must, since there is no agreed doctrine) make up his own mind on the relative weight to be given to these features, both in general and in a particular case. We can therefore say that judgments in this sphere can be rational or reasonable and hence in a sense grounded, but not that they can be proven or demonstrated.

Two consequences follow from this subjectivity in the appraisal of art. The first is that we cannot very readily speak of *knowing* that a work of art is good or bad. A person is said to be educated, not because he knows that Beethoven is a finer composer than Brahms and can say why, but rather because he holds *some* view about them (there is no one 'correct' view) and can put up a good case for it. The second consequence is that unlike the scientific cases it is impossible to distinguish between knowing how to appraise and actually doing so, since an individual will not have the complete tools for appraisal until he commits himself to certain value-judgments and so begins appraising. Thus in order to know how to appraise a picture, it is not enough to look at pictures and be able to say 'People talk about balance and proportion and vividness of colour, don't they?' in a detached fashion. He will not grasp what it is to apply these considerations until he begins to do so for himself.

The requirement that knowledge by acquaintance of works of art be accompanied by *understanding* is in many ways rather different from the corresponding requirement for knowledge *that*. In the earlier case the stress was mainly on understanding why and understanding implications: understanding concepts played a less important part. But in the case of understanding works of art some notion of 'understanding the idea of it', corresponding to conceptual understanding, is paramount. Understanding *why* a work of art was produced may be of relevance in understanding the 'idea' of it (how far this is so, and in what sense, is notoriously controversial) but apart from this it is a question about history rather than art. Understanding its *implications* (whether this means understanding its importance for art, or its message for life, if any) seems either comparatively unimportant, or part of understanding the idea.

What then do we mean by understanding the idea of a work of art? A great variety of different kinds of understanding can be brought under this general heading. At the lowest level, there is the understanding of such things as the words of a poem if they are obscure, or a grasp of the metaphors employed; in the case of a picture, the understanding of what it represents or what is symbolized by items in it, and so on. In music perhaps some degree of apprehension of the overall form of the piece is a corresponding level of understanding, or of what various passages 'represent' in a piece of 'programme music'. Beyond this there can be greater or less understanding of what the artist is 'getting at' or 'trying to do': what mood or emotion he wishes to convey, what moral he wishes to draw, what kind of impression he wishes to make – or makes, whether or not he wishes it – and so on. Understanding what an artist is getting at is to some extent independent of the 'lower' levels of understanding: thus a reader may grasp the mood of despair in a poem without fully understanding the words, or a viewer sense the grim menace 'behind' a picture without knowing the story which it depicts.

It will be seen at once that this account of understanding in the arts is extremely cursory, partly because it is very difficult to say anything which will apply to all the arts, partly because the whole field is extremely controversial – the question which we hinted at, of how far an artist's intentions are relevant in understanding his work, is only one of many problems here. But there are two general points we might make before leaving this vexed topic. Firstly, understanding in the sphere of the arts, unlike understanding in the sphere of knowledge *that*, seems to involve some measure of sympathy with or attunement to the works of art. In this respect it is rather like understanding a person; and, as with understanding a person, the distinction between understanding and liking is not always a sharp one. Secondly, there is often no objective test for deciding between failure to understand and difference in interpretation: one critic can say 'He brought out as never before the underlying wistfulness in this sonata', and another 'Anyone who thinks this a sad piece simply does not understand it' and neither can be proved wrong. It follows from this latter point that it is very much a matter of opinion, beyond a basic level, how far a given person understands the works of art which he knows.

We turn now to a brief discussion of the inclinations of the educated man in the sphere of the arts. Do we hold, firstly, that the educated man must possess the analogue of the critical disposition we discussed earlier, an inclination to look at the pictures he comes across (and perhaps also the furniture and the fashions and the domestic utensils) with an appraising rather than a non-committal eye? Here we seem to be crossing the border between the concepts of the educated and the cultivated or cultured person. The same seems to be the case when we ask whether the educated person is necessarily inclined to be 'curious' about works of art, in the sense of being keen to add to his acquaintance of them; the man who can live in a city for years without going to see its cathedral or its art gallery is not so much uneducated as uncultured. But it is not clear that this distinction in terminology is an important one; a teacher would normally aim at conveying not only the skill of appraisal but also the love of painting, poetry or whatever as such. He would also hope that in stimulating this interest in art he would develop in his pupils an awareness such that art affects their other perceptions or becomes 'part of them'. This is the analogue in the sphere of acquaintance with the arts to the inclination to *apply* knowledge *that*.

In many ways the learning of aesthetic appreciation provides close parallels with moral and religious education. Thus a man is educated, not in that he knows that adultery is wrong or that Christianity is true (if he claims to know these things it is a sign of *lack* of education, since these are not the kinds of thing which can be known in quite the ordinary sense) but in that he holds a view one way or the other on these questions and knows how to defend it. It may be objected here that in morality at least there are some basic positions which are so well established that there can be said to be a correct view: for example, that people are important. But suppose someone held that people are *not* important, and could defend this view persuasively; we would not say that his education was thereby lacking, even though we disagreed with his position. Of course, we may try to instil a certain view of morals or religion into our pupils, but if we are teaching them how to defend their views (and otherwise we are not educating them) we have given them the capacity to argue and so to disagree. The question which remains is whether there are some views which cannot be rationally defended, and whether this implies that a person who holds them cannot be called educated. We have no space to discuss this question here.

We have said a good deal about aesthetic appreciation but nothing at all about creative work (such as painting or writing) or interpretative work (such as music or acting). Yet these all play a large part in school curricula. Is a person not educated unless he takes part in such activities (or at least has acquired the capacity and the inclination to do so)? As before, it seems more natural to associate such pursuits with being cultured or cultivated than with being educated, although teachers may well aim at making their pupils cultivated in this sense. But it should be noted that this is not the only possible aim in promoting such activities at school; they can be seen as aids to aesthetic appreciation and thus be a part of education in our sense, or they can be viewed as skills which will enrich leisure, and hence as conducive to a complementary aim of education.

Our discussion in this section and the previous one has covered most of the kinds of thing taught in schools. We have suggested that the educated person, the end-product aimed at in education, possesses certain kinds of knowledge *that*, a certain kind of understanding of his knowledge *that*, certain kinds of knowledge *how* (or skills in grounding, defending or criticizing the knowledge *that*), and a certain knowledge *by acquaintance* of the arts. We have also considered how far the educated person possesses various inclinations as well as various capacities, finding that whereas a disposition to apply knowledge *that* and to be critical and curious about it seemed part of educatedness, it was more natural to call their analogues in the aesthetic sphere marks of culture rather than educatedness, although the distinction was not a sharp one.

There remain three types of curriculum subject which do not fit into our discussion so far: languages, physical education, and 'practical' subjects such as cookery or woodwork. By 'languages' we mean not those aspects which have already been covered under the head of the knowledge and appreciation of literature but the actual learning of language itself. It may be said that this is simply a means to the aesthetic ends of the literature. But we would not necessarily think learning something of a language a waste of time even if we read no literature in it. Or it might be said that languages are useful but we would consider a man who knew no foreign language uneducated, even if all foreigners spoke English to an extent which made learning their languages practically speaking unnecessary. The possibility which remains is that knowing a foreign language (a kind of knowledge which is in some ways like knowledge *that*, in some ways like knowledge *how*, in some ways like knowledge *by acquaintance*) is a special kind of mode of awareness with its own importance. It might be suggested, for instance, that through learning a foreign language we become self-conscious about language as such, in a way we never could merely by means of our own. We become able to think of it as a man-made entity separate from the things it describes, and moreover to see that it is possible to categorize things in the world in ways rather different from those enshrined in our own language, which can come to seem inevitable.

We have already indicated some of the complexities in the idea of physical education in our introductory chapter. These complexities arise from the fact that the subject can be regarded in different ways and taught in different ways. The tendency nowadays, however, is to broaden the scope of what used to be simply 'P.T.' and to connect it with other academic subjects such as physiology or indeed aesthetic appreciation; and to the extent that it moves in this direction it is moving into the central area of education, becoming a part of the intrinsic aim, rather than remaining simply as an ancillary or complementary aim. Even if it is subsumed under the latter aims, however, it still remains a very important part of the curriculum, because a trained and healthy body is a necessary condition of the achievement of continuing progress in the cognitive sphere. Woodwork similarly can be regarded from more than one point of view depending on how it is taught, and the same is true of cookery.[1]

It is worth stressing once more, however, that it does not follow from the fact that something is not part of the intrinsic aim of education that it ought not to be included as a school subject. We have chosen to give the concept of education a narrow cognitive analysis, and it therefore follows that not all that goes on in schools or universities is education. But the other activities which go on might be important ones although they are not part of the intrinsic aim of education as we have described it. Indeed, it may be easier to justify socially the expenditure of public money on some of these other activities than on education itself. It would have been possible, although less desirable, to call everything that goes on in schools and universities 'education', using the word as an umbrella, and then the problem would have become that of justifying certain

[1] Peters, op. cit., ch. IV, sect. 4.

aspects of education thus broadly conceived as against others. We believe that it is preferable to use a more restricted concept of education and then to compare education with other aims all of which may be pursued in a school.

Having tried to establish the aim of the teacher *qua* teacher we can now pass on to a consideration of the sort of skill which is essential to him.

3 Teaching as a skill-job

If the intrinsic aim of the teacher is the educated man, conceived as the man who has the relevant knowledge and understanding and the accompanying inclinations, then the skills possessed by the teacher *qua* teacher must be those which are most conducive to the production of knowledge, understanding and inclinations so conceived. Let us now consider what it is possible to say about these skills.

It must be stressed straightaway that there is no one skill or even set of skills which a teacher logically must have; rather he requires a very large number of different skills. For example, he requires the humble but important skill of being able to write on the blackboard, or the skill of being able to detect incipient restlessness (or mutiny) in his class. Again, he might be the better of having the skill of the story-teller, or that of being able to see a contemporary application of mathematical ideas or historical events which will make them seem exciting or relevant to his pupils. Clearly this list could be enormously increased, and the good teacher will possess a large number of such skills and will be encouraged to acquire or develop them by colleges of education or headmasters. Different skills or sets of skills in this sense will be required, depending on the subject being taught or the age and stage of the pupil. To stress the multiplicity of skills which the teacher requires is in no way to cast doubt on the claim that teaching is a skill-job, because to characterize a job as a skill-job is not necessarily to say that there is one and only one skill which defines the job. Even musicianship, the paradigm of the skill-job, involves sets of skills. Can we then make any general statements about the sets of skills which are constitutive of the teacher's job?

The suggestion which springs to mind here is that the skills are linked simply by their conduciveness to achieving the teacher's aim, the production of educatedness in the pupils. If this is correct, the question of the nature of the teacher's skills is a purely empirical one. To find out what skills constitute teaching as a skill-job (or, to put it another way, to find out what components make up the skill of teaching) we need to investigate what skills produce the results the teacher is aiming at, and this is a matter which is to some extent open to scientific experiment. It does not follow from this, however, that if a pupil does not become what we have called educated as a result of his schooling his teachers are thereby shown to be unskilled – to be in a sense 'no teachers'. For to produce an educated person depends on far more than the skill of the teacher. Various other factors play their part, such as the ability and industry of the pupil, the helpfulness or otherwise of his home background and so on. But despite these qualifications, there remains a connexion between teaching skill and the aims of teaching, such that to admire a teacher's skill is to say in effect 'That will help to make them educated other things being equal' or 'That will bring about their educatedness if anything can'. In that it has this connexion with an aim the skill of teaching differs from the skill of the musician, who need not have a further end in view.

With the principle established that the skills of the teachers are those which, other things being equal, will produce educatedness, we can go on to classify them in accordance with the different aspects of the nature of educatedness. Firstly, then, a teacher possesses skill in choosing the content of what he teaches, so that it fulfils the criteria we laid down for the knowledge *that* and knowledge *by acquaintance* of the educated person. Secondly, he possesses skill in imparting this knowledge – a skill which comprises not only skill in telling and showing, which produces apprehension at the time, but also skill in getting the knowledge *that* and knowledge *by acquaintance* remembered, by some combination of making it memorable and getting it learnt. Thirdly, he possesses skill in explaining, explaining being the process of producing understanding. How explaining is done will depend on the nature of the particular case, for as we saw understanding is a complex notion. It is therefore a family of skills, comprising such things as skill in drawing out implications, suggesting new examples, providing apt analogies or illuminating diagrams, supplying historical or biographical background and so on.

The fourth skill needed is skill in promoting the knowledge *how* aspect of educatedness – the ability to think historically, scientifically, aesthetically and so on. This skill is distinct from any we have so far mentioned. A teacher logically cannot *tell* a pupil how to think, because being able to think is not expressible in propositions. Nor can he explain how to do so – at least, not in the sense just mentioned – because being able to think is not a matter of understanding some particular thing. The skill needed here is a skill in transmitting skills. How this is done is an empirical question. But it seems to be done partly by the teacher demonstrating the exercise of the skill himself and partly by his putting pupils in the position where they can acquire it by practice: by setting projects, by *refusing* explanations at carefully selected moments, by asking questions that go beyond their present knowledge and so on.

It is sometimes said that this knowledge *how* dimension of educatedness 'cannot be taught'. But at the same time people often say 'He taught me how to be a scientist', and similar things. There are two reasons why people might say that knowledge *how* cannot be taught. One we have already mentioned: it cannot (logically) be taught in the most usual senses of 'told' or 'explained'. The second rests on an empirical point, that transmitting a skill is a more 'chancy' business than teaching facts, or even than explaining; in this respect, even more than in others, deficiency in the end-product is not necessarily a reflection on the skill of the teacher. If the verb 'to teach' is used as a success-verb, implying achievement of aim,[1] it follows that knowledge *how* often cannot be taught; but it sometimes can, and there can therefore be a skill in teaching it, that which produces it if anything will.

The same points arise in connexion with the inclinations which make up one component of educatedness. It might be said that they

[1] Ryle, op. cit., pp. 149–53.

are irrelevant to a discussion of teaching skills, on the ground that inclinations are not the kind of thing that can be taught. But is this true? It is certainly possible to say 'He taught me to love study' or 'He taught me to be curious and critical', so there must be a kind of teaching which is possible here. It is clear, however, that it is logically a very different kind of teaching from any we have so far mentioned. For inclinations logically cannot be taught in the sense of being told or shown, or in the sense of being explained, or even in the sense of being transmitted through demonstration and practice. They can (logically) be taught in the sense of being *aroused*, and the teaching skill in question is therefore that of arousing inclination. *How* this is done in practice is a more obscure matter and, as with knowledge *how*, a chancy one; perhaps they are 'caught' off a teacher who has them and shows them or perhaps they are already latent and only need fostering and directing. They can also be inhibited: if, say, the teacher tries to push the pupil on before he has grasped what is involved in or demanded by a certain subject or aspect of a subject. The pupil, as a result of this, may lose confidence in himself, feel that he does not know what is required of him or that he cannot cope, and this may in turn lead to loss of interest in the subject and loss of the incentive to persevere with it.

So far we have argued that the skills of the teacher can be defined as those which are conducive to the production of educatedness, other things being equal, and can be classified in accordance with the various aspects of educatedness. But it might be objected that it is perfectly possible to admire the skill in a piece of teaching – say an elegant and concise exposition of an obscure point in mathematics – while at the same time recognizing that it is not on this occasion conducive to the end of the teacher: 'Splendid stuff, but I'm afraid 5B won't get much out of it.' The answer to the objection is that if the admirer thinks a piece of teaching is not conducive to the education of the hearers, he logically cannot admire it as a piece of good *teaching*, though he might admire it as a piece of good mathematics, and as an exercise of the teacher's own educatedness. There are obvious qualifications here – the onlooker might say 'That *would* have been good teaching if he had been talking to 6A instead'. The onlooker must also refrain from over-hasty judgment on what 5B 'won't get much out of' – they may be able to get inspiration, if not understanding, from something which is 'above their heads' but of which they sense the quality.

A further objection to our account of the skills of the teacher might be that there are some methods which seem in some sense to be ruled out *ab initio*, without consideration of whether or not they might be conducive to education: we might instance here bribery, harsh punishment and intimidation, 'cramming' and 'parroting', not to speak of the obvious case of indoctrination – which last feature we shall not discuss in detail as it has been dealt with by many other writers.[1] If some methods can be excluded without considering results (the objector goes on) teaching skill cannot be essentially connected with conduciveness to results.

Now this objection as it stands is confused: it fails to distinguish between the thesis that some methods morally ought not to be used and the thesis that some methods cannot be considered part of a teacher's skills. It is true that we can rule out some methods on moral grounds without reference to their results. But this is different from saying that they are not part of teaching skills; this latter thesis may also be true, but in supporting it we need to refer to the ends of education. Let us briefly consider each of these points.

Firstly, then, some of the methods mentioned can be morally ruled out, as contravening the duties of the teacher either as a teacher or as a moral agent in general. We shall develop in more detail in Chapters Five and Six the nature of the teacher's duties and of the required moral attitudes to persons as such. For the present we can say briefly that since pupils are persons and therefore, to a greater or a lesser degree, rational beings they ought as far as pos-

---

[1] See, for example, John Wilson, 'Education and Indoctrination' and R. M. Hare, 'Adolescents into Adults', both in T. H. B. Hollins (editor) *Aims in Education: The Philosophic Approach* (Manchester University Press, 1964); J. P. White, 'Indoctrination', John Passmore, 'On Teaching to be Critical', both in R. S. Peters (editor) *The Concept of Education* (London, Routledge and Kegan Paul, 1967); R. F. Atkinson, 'Instruction and Indoctrination', in R. D. Archambault (editor) *Philosophical Analysis and Education* (London, Routledge and Kegan Paul, 1967); R. F. Atkinson, 'Instruction and Indoctrination', in R. D. Archambault (editor) *Philosophical Analysis and Education* (London, Routledge and Kegan Paul, 1965).

sible to be treated as such in a teaching situation. In other words, the use of psychological manipulation, mechanical repetition, etc. as the main techniques in teaching may be ruled out because it is *morally* wrong. Again, pupils have as persons a claim on the teacher's sympathy, and whereas *some* measure of compulsion is justified in the pupil's own interests (as we shall argue in Chapter Five) there is obviously a point beyond which the exercise of compulsion is morally unjustified, whether or not it is effective.

It is important not to give an unrealistic emphasis to this moral thesis about rational methods in teaching. Obviously non-rational techniques are important in teaching, and obviously it is not always possible to draw a sharp line between rational and non-rational techniques. The age of the pupils and the nature of the subject are factors, as we shall see in Chapters Five and Six. Our point would be, however, that non-rational techniques must always be preliminary or ancillary to the use of rational means, on the grounds that a basic use of non-rational means is morally wrong.

Let us now turn to the question whether the methods mentioned can be shown to be no part of a teacher's skills. We said earlier that this would need to be shown with reference to the ends of education. Now the reason why some kinds of methods seem ruled out from the start is that they are *by definition* productive of a non-educated result. Take for example the promotion of *parroting*, or getting pupils to be able to repeat verbal matter exactly whether or not they understand it: this method, which by definition ignores understanding, is by definition non-educational since understanding is an essential part of educatedness. Note that this argument does not rule out learning by rote as a teaching technique. A good deal of knowledge *that* and knowledge *by acquaintance* can be acquired this way, and where what is to be known is at least in part a verbal formula, like a poem or a proof of a theorem, rote-learning may be essential. But if rote-learning is to be counted as part of education it must not stand on its own; it must be supplemented by explanation to produce not merely knowledge but understanding. A similar argument could be provided concerning cramming, which may be defined as the inculcation of as much knowledge *that* as possible in a short time without regard to knowledge *how*.

In practice, of course, a teacher may decide that he is justified in using these non-educational methods to some degree: for example, a given group of pupils may seem incapable of acquiring much knowledge *how* in any case, so the teacher decides to teach them a lot of facts instead, for examination or other purposes. But this is to say that he has decided that there is a limit to the degree to which this group can be *educated* as distinct from being made into informed people. There are also interesting problems, both conceptual and moral, about the widespread former practice of getting children to learn poems by heart, at an age when they learn most easily by rote, long before they could understand them. The reasoning was that they thereby laid up a store for later understanding and enjoyment. But was this educational and was it morally justified?

It will be recalled that we mentioned harsh punishment and intimidation among the teaching methods which are often disapproved of. Now these were stated to be precluded on moral grounds, but we have not so far considered whether they can also be dubbed non-educational, like parroting and cramming. It might be argued that they must be, on the ground that they are coercive: one cannot *make* people learn, it will be said; they must learn for themselves. But this slogan, that one cannot make people learn, needs further examination, for various reasons. For one thing, it might suggest that any form of coercion in education is impossible, whereas most people would say that some measure of coercion is not only possible but justified. For another thing, it might suggest that if people must learn for themselves the teacher, skills and all, is redundant or even harmful. What then does it mean to say that one cannot make people learn? And how far is it true, in any sense?

First of all we should note that the word 'make' is ambiguous here. It may mean 'cause', as in 'I made him jump by dropping a book'. In this case the person who is made to do something does not choose to act. But making someone act can mean providing incentives for doing something, or disincentives for doing otherwise, as in 'I made him get up by promising him cream with his porridge' or 'I made him get up by threatening to beat him if he didn't'. In these cases the person who is 'made' does choose to act accordingly, but he would not have done so without the incentive or disincentive in question; we shall call this 'inducing him'. How far can a person be made to learn, in either of these senses?

First of all, a person cannot be made, in the sense of 'caused', to study, to commit things to memory, to listen, to work, to write essays, to read books. A person has to choose to do all these things; he can do otherwise if he chooses. This is a logical point: since all these things are voluntary actions, they must logically be done by choice. But just because these actions are all voluntary actions a person can logically be made, in the sense of 'induced', to perform them: that is, it makes sense to suppose that a person may choose to do them when he otherwise would not because of certain incentives (or disincentives from abstaining) which someone else provides. Moreover, it is empirically true that people often can in fact be induced to do academic work (subject to some qualifications which we shall mention later).

It may be said here that though a person can in fact be induced to acquire knowledge *that* and knowledge *by acquaintance* in these ways, he cannot be induced to understand what he knows. This is true, but it is a logical, not an empirical impossibility. For understanding is not something that a person can do at will; he can choose whether or not to learn a poem, but he cannot choose whether or not to understand it, since understanding is not a voluntary action. It does not follow that inducement can play no part in the acquisition of understanding. Suppose a sadistic schoolmaster says 'They understand it fast enough when I threaten them with the strap'. This is partly a grim joke, but partly serious; for often the voluntary activity of applying the mind is needed as a precondition of acquiring understanding, and so people can sometimes be induced to 'put their minds' to a problem to such effect that understanding emerges as a result. On the other hand, the pupil cannot always achieve understanding, however hard he tries; it depends partly on factors beyond his control.

Can a teacher *cause* a pupil to understand? There is no one answer to this question. Some things a teacher does seem to cause understanding of some things: for example, he draws a diagram or suggests an analogy or example, as a result of which understanding is produced immediately – 'the penny drops', as we say. But as we saw earlier this kind of process is very unpredictable, unlike making someone jump by dropping a book. This is because what makes one pupil understand will have no effect on another, depending on factors such as differences in intelligence and in 'the way the mind works'.

Strictly speaking, then, the teacher's activity here is at best a causal *factor* rather than a cause: it is not a guarantee of results, but may be an important item among the many factors contributing to understanding in a given case. If the teacher's activity is an important causal factor and the result fairly prompt, he will naturally speak of making someone understand – though it may well be that some minimum degree of activity on the part of the pupil is always necessary, if only the activity of paying attention. But where what is to be understood is rather complex, what the teacher does is only a small item in the total process of acquiring understanding. Other things necessary, apart from the requisite level of ability in the pupils, might be a voluntary activity on the pupils' part, of the kind we call 'chewing it over', 'thinking it out' and so on; various workings of the brain over which they have no control; and such things as further relevant experience or further learning. In this kind of case a teacher might say 'This isn't the kind of thing I (or anyone) can *make* you understand'. He may go on to say 'You've just got to see this for yourselves'. This is in a sense a misleading expression, as a person sees for himself even the things he is made to understand; but what is meant is that they must come to see it *by* themselves, that after the teacher's initial contribution he can do no more for them.

So far, then, we have suggested that the teacher can sometimes induce committing to memory, studying, thinking a thing over and other voluntary intellectual activities; he can sometimes cause, or contribute to the causing of, understanding. He logically cannot, however, cause a pupil to undertake intellectual activities; he logically cannot induce a pupil to understand something; he often empirically cannot cause a pupil to understand, even in the weak sense of providing an important causal condition of understanding. None of these limitations supports either the view that the teacher is redundant or the view that coercion in education is impossible.

On the first of these views, it remains an empirical question how far a given pupil can achieve certain educational results without a teacher – and, within that broad question, whether a teacher helps him to achieve the result more quickly, whether a teacher can actually be a hindrance in some cases and so on. (There is also the conceptual question of how far those vital allies of the self-educator, the authors of books, the compilers of television programmes and so on can be counted as a kind of teacher, but we shall ignore this complication.)

The second view, that coercion in education is impossible, raises mainly empirical questions also once the *logical* impossibility of coercing understanding is understood. But the questions are more complicated than we previously suggested. For there are really two kinds of empirical issue. One is the question whether particular pupils will choose, given particular incentives or disincentives, to perform particular tasks or not. The other question is subtler: how far various intellectual activities *can* be done 'to order', whether in general or by particular people. It might be retorted that it is part of the nature of an activity, distinguishing it from an involuntary happening such as a sneeze, that it can always be done to order. But this is not exactly true. There may be some activities which a given person can perform if he wants to but cannot perform against the grain, even if he chooses to try to do so and even if there are no external impediments. And common sense suggests that intellectual activities may well be in this category: a person literally cannot always concentrate on something which bores him, or learn a poem he hates, or work on a problem which repels him, even if he chooses (as a result of some inducement) to try to do so. If this is true, there comes a point (no doubt different for different people) where trying to make a person learn by coercion is useless, quite apart from the moral considerations limiting its use which we mentioned earlier. The point may well be in a different place in the case of bribery; our guess is that a child who loathes learning French verbs and is told he can have a treat if he does so is less inhibited by his hatred than a child who is told he will be punished if he does not learn them. Skill in judging these things is part of the skill of the teacher.

It may well be objected at this point that, whereas we have discussed senses in which people can and cannot be made to learn and understand, we have not touched on the inclination component of education. Can a person be made to have the inclinations which form part of educatedness? First of all, can he be induced to have them? The short answer is that inclinations, not being the kind of thing which a person can choose whether to have, logically cannot themselves be induced; and it might be added that inducing pupils to do things which they would if educated be inclined to do is precisely the way to prevent the inclinations characteristic of the educated person from developing. The latter claim is of course an empirical one; it needs confirmation by experience, but it seems plausible – until one recollects that making, in the sense of inducing, children to behave in certain ways in other spheres is supposed to promote, not inhibit, the relevant inclinations. Thus assuring polite or considerate behaviour by reward and punishment is thought to promote spontaneous good behaviour later on. Is this belief mistaken, or is the case of the moral inclinations different from that of the intellectual ones?

The reply to this question is again one for the empirical investigator rather than the philosopher, but we shall make a few tentative suggestions. We suggest that in both spheres inducement by itself cannot get very far. What the teacher and the parent both hope for in the respective spheres we have mentioned is primarily to arouse the relevant inclinations themselves. As we said earlier in the case of the educational inclinations, this might be done in both cases by example and inspiration, and by fostering the germ of inclinations already present. (We shall discuss in Chapter Six the part natural human sympathy for others plays in morality.) In this sense, the teacher may be able to make his pupils (not induce them, but cause them) to love knowledge, to cherish accuracy and so on.

But if the intellectual inclinations can be aroused in this way, why is there any need for inducement in education? We suggest there are three reasons, all of which have their parallels in the moral sphere. Firstly, because acting in the required way despite contrary inclinations can sometimes lead to a change in inclination. The teacher has to guess when being made to read Shakespeare will lead a pupil to like it and when to being 'put off' for life, just as a parent has to guess whether making his child visit a sick aunt will make him rebel later against all sick-visiting or take it up of his own accord. Secondly, because curiosity, love of accuracy, etc., even if they are present, are not necessarily the strongest impulses (as we saw even in the case of the educated man) and so their motive-power may need reinforcing by what we have called inducement if they are not to get choked in their infancy by natural sloth. Thirdly, because there are times when reward or punishment is the best way of demonstrating (and hence, it is hoped, transmitting) one's own concern. If the teacher says, or suggests, 'I won't make you do it properly if you don't want to', he runs the risk of the child's saying or thinking 'If truth or accuracy is as important as you keep saying, why are you letting this shoddy work pass?' and being disillusioned as a result. Good judgment in this matter is among a teacher's most important skills.

This discussion of the senses in which, and the extent to which, a teacher can make a pupil educated is necessarily inconclusive because so much of it relates to empirical questions. But perhaps enough has been said to show that, whereas what we have called inducement has its limitations and a quasi-automatic implantation of educatedness is impossible, there is some place for inducement in education and plenty that the teacher can do.

4 Conclusion

Insofar as teaching is a skill-job we can characterize it only in very general terms, for the skills of the teacher are manifold. But the nature of the skills is necessarily linked with the concept of educatedness itself. Insofar as teaching is an aim-job we can depict its intrinsic aim as the creation of the educated man, conceived as the man who has the knowledge, understanding and inclinations of the kind we have analysed. The point of characterizing teaching in this narrow way is to bring into sharp focus what we see as the essence, the bare bones or the Platonic Form of teaching, and it is important to do this because the many other activities which a teacher is called on to perform may well obscure this form. If we are to be able to compare and evaluate these other activities against each other and against teaching it is crucial to be able to say what each is.

Chapter Three

Justifications: intrinsic aims

We argued in Chapter One that the intrinsic aim of the teacher is education; and in Chapter Two we tried to say what education so conceived consists in and what skills the teacher logically must possess if his aim is education. We have tried to make it clear that we have been suggesting a certain content for the term 'education' which leaves it open whether or how far such a state is worth bringing about or aiming at. To consider this latter issue is to consider what we may call the justification of education, and this will be the subject of Chapters Three and Four. Now it will be remembered that in Chapter One we said that there are two possible ways of attempting to justify the pursuit of education: one is to say that education is in some sense good or worthwhile in itself, and the other to say that it is good or worthwhile on account of its extrinsic aims or ends,[1] or those other good states of affairs which are brought about through education. In this chapter we shall consider attempts to show that education is good in itself, and in the next chapter we shall examine attempts to justify education through its extrinsic aims or ends. Justifications in terms of the intrinsic aims of education are not of course incompatible with those in terms of its extrinsic aims: education might be looked at as something which is good both in itself and in its conse-

[1] In Chapters Three and Four we sometimes use the term 'end' instead of the term 'aim'. This is because the phrase 'good as an end' is traditionally used in the context of discussions of how something can be justified. But we mean the same by the terms 'aim' and 'end'.

quences. It is convenient, however, to consider the two sorts of justification separately, beginning with the arguments for the view that education is good in itself.

1 *The transcendental argument*

This type of argument was first developed by Kant in his Critical Philosophy. In general, a transcendental argument is one which seeks to establish what we must be assuming in order for certain sorts of judgment to be possible. For example, in his *Critique of Pure Reason* Kant argues that various concepts, principles and categories must be operative *a priori* for knowledge to be possible.[1] R. S. Peters, in his book *Ethics and Education*, uses a specific form of this general kind of argument to try to defend his view that intellectual pursuits, those into which education initiates people, are good in themselves.

Peters begins by arguing that if 'certain principles are necessary for a form of discourse to have meaning, to be applied or to have point'[2] then we can justify them in the sense of showing that anyone using the form of discourse is committed to them. (This is of course an *ad hominem* justification, one which is addressed only to those who use the form of discourse in question – a restriction which is more grave than Peters realizes, as we shall see.) The second stage in Peters' argument is the assertion that one such 'differentiated form of discourse'[3] is employed when people ask 'what they ought or ought not to do and when they judge things as good and bad'.[4] This form of discourse is sometimes characterized by Peters as the asking of, and the attempt to answer, the question 'Why do this rather than that?' [5] – a rather ambiguous formulation. Leaving aside

[1] For discussions of Kant's conception of the *a priori*, see A. C. Ewing, *A Short Commentary on Kant's Critique of Pure Reason*, ch. II (London, Methuen, 1938); John Kemp, *The Philosophy of Kant*, ch. I (London, Oxford University Press, Opus 36, 1968).

[2] R. S. Peters, *Ethics and Education*, p. 115 (London, Allen and Unwin, 1966).

[3] Peters, op. cit., p. 114.   [4] Peters, op. cit., loc. cit.

[5] Peters, op. cit., p. 154 et passim.

for the present a difficulty, to which we shall return, about the words 'Why do . . .?', there is also the fact that 'Why do this rather than that?' might mean either 'Why do any one thing rather than any other?' (a general scepticism about norms in behaviour) or 'Why do (say) poetry rather than pushpin?' (a more specific question about the value of some particular activity). On the whole Peters seems to have the latter meaning in mind, and he is moreover imagining not a sceptic about poetry so much as a serious inquirer wondering what one ought to do in life and weighing up possibilities in his effort to find out. But the problem of justifying the pursuit of education obviously arises even more acutely if one is speaking to the general sceptic, and so we shall ask finally whether Peters' argument can deal with such a sceptic, as well as with the serious inquirer we described.

The third stage in Peters' argument is to suggest that a person who asks seriously the question 'Why do this rather than that?'[1] is committed to the pursuit of the kinds of inquiry which are involved in education. In other words, a man who is weighing up the value of various possible pursuits, including the intellectual pursuits involved in education, is, by virtue of the very asking, committed to the latter pursuits: when he reflects about the worth of this or that activity he 'will find himself embarking upon those forms of inquiry such as science, history, literature and philosophy which are concerned with the description, explanation and assessment of different forms of human activity'.[2]

Let us now consider some problems in Peters' argument. The first problem is concerned with the *ad hominem* nature of the transcendental argument to which we drew attention earlier. It is a justification only to those who already ask 'Why do this rather than that?' Now Peters of course admits this limitation, which is part of the very notion of a transcendental deduction. But he seems not to see how serious a limitation it is. It is a serious limitation because it is easy, and common, for people to avoid raising this question at all. Indeed Peters himself says: 'It is surprising . . . how many people are strangers to this attitude [a non-instrumental and disinterested one] . . . Their way of life over and above those things they do

[1] Peters, op. cit., p. 161.   [2] Peters, op. cit., p. 162.

because of their station and its duties, because of general social rules, and because of palpable considerations of their interest, is largely the outcome of habit, social pressure, sympathy and attraction towards what is immediately pleasurable.'[1]

It might, however, be denied that this is a serious limitation in practice, on the grounds that it is very difficult for people to avoid raising questions about their moral duties, and that questions about moral duties presuppose questions about what is worthwhile or good in itself. After all (the objection goes on) one of our duties must surely be to promote what is good in itself; how then can we discourse about our duties without investigating what this good is? The objector concludes that, contrary to our view, it is difficult *not* to raise questions about what is good in itself.

But this objection is ill-founded. We may grant that it is psychologically difficult for people to opt out of all discourse about moral duties – since, however amoral they want to be, they are almost sure to want occasionally to say that someone morally ought to do something – though it is not psychologically *impossible* to opt out in this way, let alone illogical. We may also grant that a really careful and exhaustive investigation of what one's duties are may well logically presuppose forming some notion of what is good in itself. But in practice people, although they discourse about their duties, often do not work things out to an extent which leads them to realize the relevance of the good in itself. Thus they may see duty solely in terms of rules and roles, and problems about duty in terms of conflicts between rules or roles – 'my station and its duties', as Peters (quoting Bradley) says above.[2] If they have a notion beyond this, of promoting good in general, they may well see this good in terms simply of what people want, and not raise the question whether what people want is necessarily a good thing at all. We conclude then that one cannot argue from the likelihood of duty-discourse to the likelihood of discourse about what is good in itself, and hence that the limitation in scope of the possible recipients of Peters' justification still remains.

[1] Peters, op. cit., p. 154.
[2] F. H. Bradley, *Ethical Studies*, 'My Station And Its Duties' (Oxford University Press, Oxford Paperbacks, edited by Richard Wollheim, 1962).

The second problem is one which Peters mentions but does not see as a problem. He says that the man who asks 'Why do this rather than that?' has 'embarked upon a difficult and almost endless quest'[1] because the 'this' and 'that' of the question are conceived differently according to the nature and the degree of one's education. This is presumably a corollary of Peters' 'initiation' view of education: just as (it might be maintained) the non-believer cannot really understand the nature of religion from outside and the novice has a different view of it from the long-established practiser, so the non-educated person cannot understand, because he does not share, the form of life which intellectual pursuits comprise. The main difficulty inherent in this position is as follows: will there ever come a point at which the inquirer can reasonably say 'Now I know enough about science, philosophy and art (through doing them) to answer finally the question whether they are worth doing'? If so, the transcendental deduction seems to yield only the principle that one cannot meaningfully ask what one should do in life without some (unspecified) degree of education; which may be true enough, but is not what Peters wants, and furnishes no reason for trying to get any more education than that amount. If not, the original question is unanswerable, and the attempt to answer it pointless.

Peters would reply here that we have misunderstood the nature of his argument. He is not (or not mainly) asserting a temporal thesis, that we cannot understand the value of these activities until such time as we have some experience of them. Indeed, this would not be a transcendental argument. His thesis is rather a logical one: that engaging in the activities is presupposed in the very attempt to assess the value of them. But we can then raise a third difficulty: if this is true, in what sense is it a *justification* of the activities? To see what is meant here, consider a trivial analogy. The activity of asking questions is presupposed in asking the question 'Why ask questions?' and this seems to show that the question is self-answering in some way. But this fact does not show that it is *valuable* to ask questions. Similarly, if, as Peters suggests, asking and answering the question 'Why do this rather than that?' presupposes the undertaking of some form of rational inquiry, it is a self-answering

[1] Peters, op. cit., p. 161.

question. But this fact does not show that rational inquiry is *valuable* which is what Peters wants to show.

Peters does not see this difficulty because of the ambiguous wording of his argument. As we saw earlier, he expresses the basic question as 'Why do this rather than that?' Apart from the difficulties mentioned earlier, the basic 'Why do . . .?' itself can mean either 'Shall I do this or that?' or 'Why is this more valuable than that?' (Similarly he speaks of those who ask the question as being 'committed' to theoretical activities, which can mean either 'committed to undertaking them' or 'committed to valuing them highly'.) It is the second question which he is trying to answer, but it is the *first* question which presupposes commitment (in the first sense) to inquiry.

The only move now open to Peters is to retreat to a weaker thesis. He could say that his aim is not to show the value of theoretical activities but simply to get people to undertake them, and that this more modest aim is achieved if he can show the questioner that because of his questioning he is already committed to performing them. But is even this aim achieved? If the questioner is in fact a general sceptic of the kind mentioned earlier, sceptical about the point of any kind of thinking at all, why should he not reply to Peters: 'I see I am contradicting myself in asking in a serious and inquiring frame of mind whether there is any point in inquiry; henceforth I shall reject all questioning and simply drift along mindlessly'? If, on the other hand, the questioner is asking, not about thinking as such, but about the particular forms of inquiry involved in education, Peters has to show that even asking 'What ought one to do?' commits him to undertaking these. This is indeed what Peters maintains, but it seems to be true only to a very limited extent, far short of the scope of education.

Let us enlarge briefly on this last point. It may be true that some 'human' subjects, such as history, sociology or psychology, include within them material which helps us to understand the place of theoretical inquiry in man's life. It is also of course true that philosophy itself includes the examination of questions such as 'What is the nature of science?' and 'What is the value of science?' But it is difficult to see how geography or mathematics can throw light upon the nature of theoretical inquiry. Even in the case of the subjects which *do* throw light on the questioner's problem, the degree of them which he is thereby committed to doing is far too slight to meet the conditions for education: for example, to understand the different ways in which scientists, say, may view their work is only a very small portion of psychology, and to understand how science began a very small portion of history.

We conclude, then, that whatever may be said of transcendental arguments in general, Peters has not succeeded in providing a transcendental justification of the pursuit of education. The most he has done is to show that those who already ask, in a serious frame of mind, 'What ought one to do in life?' are thereby committed to undertaking some small part of the theoretical activities characteristic of the educated man.

2 *Education as good in itself*

It may plausibly be maintained that appeals to complicated forms of argument, of the kind we have just considered and rejected, are beside the point when attempting to justify education. The simplest justification for education which can be offered – and perhaps the one which in the final showing is the most satisfactory – is that its intrinsic aims, those states of mind which constitute it, are good in themselves or desirable for their own sakes. If it be asked how we can know this the reply is that many people, in every age, have claimed to see it to be so – in other words our appeal is to what would now be called intuition. Of course, the details of the content would vary from age to age but the general idea – that a cultivated mind, or the possession of knowledge and understanding, are goods in themselves – is a very widespread one with a long history. Whether we can strictly speak of *knowledge* based on such an intuition is, however, rather doubtful, since there seem to be no ways of checking it or verifying it; we should speak instead of 'faith' or 'conviction'.[1] This limitation is inherent in the nature of the case.

[1] See R. S. Downie and Elizabeth Telfer, *Respect For Persons*, pp. 148–9 (London, Allen and Unwin, 1969).

We can show that something is good as a *means* by showing empirically that it promotes some desired or desirable end; but this line of argument does not apply to things which are good as ends. The most we can do is to remove possible misunderstandings of the view that educatedness is good in itself and seek to meet objections to it.

The first objection we shall consider is to the whole notion of the good in itself: it might be said that nothing is in fact good *in itself*, since its goodness depends on the value put on it by human beings. But this objection, which we may call the 'subjectivist' objection, is ambiguous; we shall discuss each possible meaning separately. The first possibility is that 'good in itself' is simply a misleading phrase for 'desired as an end' or 'desired for its own sake'. But in fact we can fairly clearly distinguish the idea of a thing's being good in itself from the idea of its being desired for its own sake. Thus a thing can be desired for its own sake without even the desirer thinking it good in itself – for example, another's suffering. If a person sees something as good in itself this means that he *values* it: he thinks it ought to be desired for itself, whether or not it is so desired.

Of course the people who regard education, or anything else, as good in itself very often do also desire it for itself; perhaps, indeed, they necessarily do, though we need not go into that thorny problem. But its goodness is not seen as depending on their desiring. On the contrary, they will see it as making a kind of claim on them quite independent of their actual desires: 'Whatever you do want, this is what you ought to want.' This is not to say that *no* justification connected with actual wants is possible. The most plausible attempts at such justifications, however, are in terms of the pleasure, satisfaction or happiness produced by a thing; in other words, they present it as good not in itself but in its consequences. We shall consider in our next chapter how far education may be justified in this way.

Those who espouse the subjectivist objection in the *second* sense would grant that we can, as just argued, distinguish valuing a thing from wanting it. But they still maintain that nothing can be good *in itself*, in the sense of having intrinsic value. In their view, such a phrase is simply a misleading way of saying that many people (or the speaker) value it, i.e. regard it in a particular way, as though it had some kind of claim on them. To suppose that a thing's goodness belongs to *it*, rather than to how people regard it (the objection goes on), is to presuppose something like an objective order of values which exists independently of the ideas of human beings; and such a view is too mystic and metaphysical to be acceptable. We have no room here to consider all the implications of this objection. (We have discussed elsewhere a non-naturalist view of morality, a view which is of course similar in kind to the view under discussion about the good in itself.)[1] For present purposes we can simply reiterate that some people seem to *believe* that some things are worth desiring and pursuing for their own sakes, and moreover regard this not merely as a psychological quirk about themselves but as reflecting an independent validity; and whereas they may be wrong or confused about a particular case it seems implausible to suppose that this general psychological phenomenon, which lays claim to the existence of objective values in things, is entirely based on illusion.

Our claim, then, is that it is after all plausible to suppose that some things are good in themselves, in the sense that they possess an intrinsic value. It remains true, as we said in the previous section, that many people who have a notion of duty nevertheless do not think much in terms of the good in itself, even though some notion of the good in itself seems to be required for any exhaustive consideration of one's duties.

A second objection to our position is aimed not at the general conception of the good in itself but at our assertion that education in particular is among such goods. The objection is that our conception of the intrinsic aims of education seems to suggest that what is worthwhile in the intellectual sphere is a life spent on research, and this is not open to most people.

Now one way of dealing with this objection would be to say that a thing's not being attainable by most people does not preclude it from being good in itself; perhaps there are certain goods which only a favoured few can acquire. But we need not take this line, since we would in any case wish to deny the premise on which the objection is based: that our account of educatedness suggests that it

[1] Downie and Telfer, op. cit., pp. 144–52.

is a life of research which is worthwhile in itself. It is true that our account suggests that the educated person will engage in intellectual activity. For although we depicted educatedness itself as a state, the combination of capacities and inclinations which we attributed to it must logically issue in relevant activity, other things being equal, just like any other inclination to do a thing combined with the capacity to do it. But intellectual activity is not the same as intellectual occupation, and the intellectual activities characteristic of the educated man are not confined to the calling of the researcher; they can be carried out in any sphere of life. An educated man who chooses (or is forced) to spend all his time in occupations which do not 'use his mind' at all is not thereby prevented from exercising his knowledge *how*, his knowledge *that*, his critical disposition and his curiosity. If, for example, he finds himself working at a conveyor belt in a factory, he will *qua* educated person be disposed to weigh up the explanation given by the foreman of why the belt sometimes sticks, and if the explanation seems implausible he will be inclined to try to find out the real reason. Hence some form of the intellectual activities which are the manifestations of the state of educatedness is open to everyone, whatever his lot; we need not follow Aristotle and portray the man who exercises his theoretical intellect as a kind of mystic with private means,[1] even if we grant the obvious point that some ways of life offer purer and more unfettered opportunities than others to use one's education.

It should be added here that our example of a man who must spend all his time in a manner which does not require him to use his mind is unnecessarily pessimistic. Whatever jobs people find themselves forced to do in these days of job-shortage, leisure can still be the opportunity to pursue activities worthwhile in themselves. Indeed Aristotle looked on work as the means to leisure,[2] and it may be that with increased leisure the exercise of those qualities possessed by the educated man will be seen more clearly to have the intrinsic worth we have been claiming for them.

The third objection we shall consider is that our thesis involves an over-intellectual view of life and ignores the fact that ordinary

[1] Aristotle, *Nicomachean Ethics*, X, chapters 7 and 8.
[2] Aristotle, op. cit., 1177b5.

people regard many things as desirable in themselves besides those we have been regarding as the intrinsic aims or ends of education. This idea is based on a misunderstanding of our position, because we are by no means committed to the thesis that the intrinsic ends of education are the only ends good in themselves, or even that they are in any sense the 'highest' of such goods. It is quite consistent with our position to maintain that love, friendship, religious experience, morality, are all good as ends or even 'higher' than the intrinsic ends of education. Moreover, it will be remembered that we include aesthetic appreciation in its widest sense among the ends of education, and hence we are not taking a narrowly intellectual approach to education.

The final objection to our view that educatedness can be justified by saying that it is a good in itself is that it is not clear that an intrinsic good must always be regarded as taking precedence over an instrumental good. If therefore the situation is such at present that we have to choose between education and instrumental goods of paramount urgency and importance, is it clear that education is at the moment justified at all? And in fact (the argument goes on) we do have to choose in this way. Governments have to decide whether to spend resources on education or on housing and hospitals; those choosing a career have to decide whether to spend their lives in educating or in doing something undeniably 'useful', like medicine; children have to decide whether to go on with their education or to do something 'to help the world'; students have to decide whether to spend their vacations educating themselves or going on work camps.

The answer to this difficulty is threefold. First of all, education is useful as well as good in itself. It may be thought that this is quite obvious. But whereas it is clear that training in practical skills is useful, and also that science (and social science) is useful, it is not *obvious* that education as a whole is useful – we hope to show that it is so in the last section of Chapter Four. Secondly, even if education had no instrumental value, its nature is not such that it can be postponed till the world's problems are sorted out. If we did this, we would break the tradition and be left with no one able to pass on the forms of thought which make up education. Thirdly, it is no always possible to be useful. It is easy to find oneself assuming that there is always something which can be done about a problem, but while this is doubtless a good working maxim it is not a necessary truth. Still less is it the case that we can always know that a particular person, or a particular use of resources, will be useful rather than harmful in a particular context. Supposing a teacher of philosophy decides to leave off teaching philosophy and become a social worker, or suppose the local authority diverts some of its library and museum funds into building high-rise flats: is it clear that more good than harm is done? If therefore it be granted that education is an intrinsic good, it is often a surer benefit to pursue than putative instrumental goods – though admittedly the uncertainty of instrumental goodness is very much a matter of degree.

We have tried to provide some defence of our view that educatedness is a state worthwhile in itself and that this is a sufficient justification of it (whatever *other* justifications may be provided by its extrinsic ends). It is still the case, of course, that this position depends entirely on an intuitive judgment. For those who remain unconvinced by this judgment, recourse to another form of argument will be required, if such can be found. We shall now consider one such possibility.

3 Educatedness and self-realization: a redescription argument

One way of showing that educatedness is a good in itself, or worth aiming at for its own sake, might be by means of a 're-description' in terms of some concept already viewed as describing a good-in-itself. If, for example, we suggest that educatedness is good in itself because the educated man is properly to be seen as one who fulfils the function of man, or contributes to his self-realization, or manifests the divine element in man, we are using such an argument. It is clearly not an appeal to good consequences; it works by portraying the thing to be discussed as an example (or perhaps *the* example) of a type of thing which it is hoped the hearer already accepts as good in itself. Thus if a person already thinks of fulfilling the function of a human being as something good in itself, he can be convinced that education is good in itself if he can be convinced that it is a way (or *the* way) of fulfilling one's function.

It might be objected that redescription arguments are open to the same difficulty as we encountered in the previous section: that our position in the end simply rests on an intuitively based judgment. For it might be said that to redescribe education in terms of something else – fulfilling one's function, say – is still to leave us with an intuitive judgment, that whatever the redescription is in terms of is good in itself. This must be granted, but we can reply by pointing out that the redescription form of argument does not *impose* an intuitive judgment on the hearer, but rather appeals to one he himself is already inclined to make. In other words, we are imagining an objector who is unconvinced that understanding or knowledge are good in themselves, and we are attempting to convince him by redescribing these intrinsic ends of education in terms of some other concept which for him already indicates something good in itself.

We shall examine the possibilities of a redescription argument in terms of the concept of self-realization. It may be that we can redescribe the state of educatedness in such a way that it can be seen to be the same as the state of self-realizedness. In other words if we can show that the educated man and the self-realized man are one and the same, then if we assume, as it is natural to do, that self-realization is a state which does not require further justification we have *ipso facto* shown that educatedness does not require further justification – that it is good as an end or worth having for its own sake. What then is it for a person to achieve self-realization? Presumably a person achieves self-realization when he fulfils his nature as a person, so we must consider the question of the nature of a person, or, in Mill's phrase, the 'distinctive endowment of a human being'.[1]

Before we try to answer this question, however, we should become clear about what kind of question it is. It is not merely an investigation into what distinguishes humans from other animals. This can be seen by considering whether we would call such things

[1] J. S. Mill, *On Liberty*, ch. III, p. 187 (London, Collins, The Fontana Library, edited by Mary Warnock, 1962).

as differences in the number and type of teeth, or in the way hair is distributed on the body, part of the 'distinctive endowment' of a human being. Rather we are looking for the most important difference between humans and other animals, where 'important' indicates an *evaluative* judgment which picks out certain features rather than others (as the evaluative word 'endowment' suggests). It may seem that we are simply analysing the concept of a person in an evaluatively neutral manner. But the concept of a *person* is already an evaluative concept with something of the force of 'that which makes a human being valuable' implied in it, and this is even more true of the more abstract concept 'personality'. As we shall see in Chapter Six, to regard someone as a person, or as having personality, is to think of him as an appropriate object of some attitudes, an inappropriate object of some others: and this is because the notion of a 'person' carries with it evaluative force.[1]

Traditionally it has been assumed that basic to the distinctive endowment of a human being is his reason, and we accept the traditional assumption and shall try to explain our own version of it. We hold in the first place that reason has a theoretical aspect. This aspect of reason we have already discussed in our previous chapter: theoretical reason is that which enables a person to acquire understanding and the three forms of knowledge which were described in that chapter. Rather than say more on theoretical reason we propose here to discuss the practical aspects of reason, aspects which Kant identified by his concept of 'rational will'. What then is involved in 'rational will', or the practical aspect of reason?

It involves, in the first place, the ability to choose for oneself and, more extensively, to formulate purposes, plans and policies of one's own. A second and closely connected element is the ability to carry out decisions, plans or policies without undue reliance on the help of others. These two abilities are connected by a kind of pragmatic necessity, in that the ability to decide requires for its development the concurrent development of the ability to execute. The importance we attach to these manifestations of the rational will is reflected in our firm approval of such traits of character as 'being able to stand on one's own feet', 'being relatively independent of

[1] See Downie and Telfer, op. cit., pp. 19–23.

others', 'sticking to one's guns', 'knowing what one wants, or what one ought to do', 'knowing one's own mind' and 'being able to decide for oneself'. To help a child to develop these traits is seen as 'helping him to become a person in his own right'. Conversely, to impair a person's abilities to formulate and carry out aims and policies of his own devising is to that extent to destroy him as a person. This can happen, for example, to a person who is injured physically or mentally if friends help him too much. The development of personality can also be blocked on a larger scale by political arrangements which restrict the range of images which people can form of themselves. The exercises of the rational will involved in the foregoing examples are expressions of what may be called the ability to be self-determining. It is clearly important in any analysis of what is valuable in human personality.

But there is a second feature – much stressed by Kant – involved in the possession of a rational will: the ability to govern one's conduct by rules, and indeed, more grandly, to adopt rules which one holds to be binding on oneself and all rational beings. This feature of the exercise of rational will is the one which most clearly distinguishes man from animals, for whereas some animals may possess to a slight extent the ability to carry out plans of their own devising – or at least to act in ways which invite the use of such language – it is not plausible to suggest that they can have a conception of a rule, far less adopt rules for themselves. The ability to shape one's conduct in terms of rules and to adopt (or even create) rules valid for all men is called by Kant the autonomy of the will, and in the autonomy of the will Kant sees the very essence of personality.

It might be objected that the analysis of the characteristic human endowment has not yet mentioned emotions, feelings or desires. Yet they surely contribute something of distinctive value to human personality. Now it would be unfair to Kant to say that he saw no value at all in sentience, but he certainly did not see it as contributing anything to the intrinsic worth of a person; this he restricted to the exercise of reason in a narrow sense. But it may be that the sharp distinction between reason and sentience accepted by Kant and other philosophers is artificial. Sentience in the form in which it is characteristic of a person does involve reason. It is true that some animals may be able to experience certain emotions, but the ability to feel and express a wide range of sustained emotions is characteristically human, and it involves the perception and discrimination which only reason can supply. We can see this if we consider how the anger or fear of a person differs from its counterpart in an animal. Hence to see the value of the human person as lying partly in the ability to experience emotion is not to say anything which is inconsistent with the exercise of reason; for insofar as emotions are characteristically human they necessarily involve reason. In a similar way, the experiencing of complex desires involves reason. The exercise of reason is to be seen, then, as something at once (in old-fashioned terminology) cognitive, conative and affective, and it is the ability to exercise it in theoretical reasoning, self-determination and rule-following which gives human personality its distinctive nature.

If we assume that this characterization of the nature of a person is roughly acceptable we can now raise the question of whether the state of educatedness will constitute the realization or fulfilment of this nature.[1] But what do we mean by 'self-realization'? We are certainly not claiming to expound the technical term 'self-realization' as it appears in the works of specific philosophers such as F. H. Bradley.[2] Our aim rather is to try to catch hold of vaguer more popular notions to which ordinary people appeal, not necessarily under that title, when discussing the aims of education or indeed of life in general. These ideas are of course not very sharply defined, so any attempt to impose definition on them involves a certain arbitrary drawing of outlines – we hope not too arbitrary to do some justice to an important cluster of ideas.

'Realization', in this context, clearly does not mean what it more normally means, viz. 'becoming aware'; for no one who talks about self-realization would allow that what he really means is something

[1] For another discussion of this topic, see Elizabeth Telfer, 'Education and Self-Realization', *Proceedings of the Philosophy of Education Society of Great Britain*, Supplementary Issue, 1972.

[2] F. H. Bradley, *Ethical Studies*, 'Why Should I Be Moral?', et passim (Oxford University Press, Oxford Paperbacks, edited by Richard Wollheim, 1962).

like self-knowledge, however valuable he may admit the latter to be. The relevant sense of 'realization' is that of 'becoming real' or 'actualization'. In one sense, of course, a self or person is real already, but we can see how this idea of realization applies to him if we say that his reason, both theoretical and practical, incorporates a mass of potentialities which may or may not be realized. Self-realization is a process whereby some aspects of this potentiality become actualized or made real.

We can give this idea more precision by distinguishing two kinds of potentiality, and also two ways in which these two potentialities may become realized. The two kinds of potentiality relevant to our purposes we shall call *capacities* and *inclinations*; a capacity is a skill which enables a person to produce a certain kind of result if he chooses; an inclination is a tendency to try to do a certain kind of thing (with greater or less success). The two ways in which these potentialities may be realized are *exercise* and *development*. I exercise my capacity for cooking in actually using my skill. Again, I exercise my inclination to read poetry in actually choosing to do so. In both these examples a part of me which is sometimes latent is being actually employed. But we can also realize both kinds of potentiality in developing them, either from scratch or from an embryonic existence. Thus I can acquire or increase a capacity for writing poetry or an inclination for rock-climbing. Here I am not just manifesting a potentiality which is there all the time, but sometimes latent; I am also in a sense extending myself or creating a new potentiality. In this latter case, the potentialities are realized, not all at once in actions, but gradually in the creation of a new or increased potentiality. If we see self-realization in terms of the *exercise* of potentialities, we are depicting it as acting in certain ways, whereas if we see it in terms of the *developing* of potentialities, we are depicting it as becoming a certain kind of person.

These two kinds of realization are of course closely linked in practice. For one thing, we normally develop or cultivate potentialities by exercising them. Thus I become a skilled poet – developing a larger poetic self, as it were – by exercising what talent in this direction I already have. Again, we normally cultivate potentialities in order to exercise them; it would be odd to develop a skill in writing poetry and then never write any. But the fact remains that we can make the conceptual distinction, and we shall find that the distinction is reflected in the ways in which various educational processes are conceived.

So far, then, we have analyzed self-realization as comprising two different ways of actualizing the two different kinds of potentiality which a person has: we may call this the *form* of self-realization. It seems that this formal structure of self-realization fits well the formal structure of educatedness. Thus, the educated person was said to have certain capacities and certain inclinations. In terms of its formal properties, then, self-realization can feature in a redescription of the state of educatedness. But to show that the *form* of self-realization can be applied to educatedness is not sufficient for a justifying redescription of educatedness. We must show that the *content* of educatedness is such that it realizes – exercises or develops – the main features of the self, or of the distinctive endowment of a person, as we have earlier described it.

Now there is clearly no difficulty at all about saying that educatedness realizes the aspects of the person involving theoretical reason. Indeed, this might almost seem true by definition. A man is called 'educated' insofar as he has acquired the capacities for the different forms of thought and awareness of which the human mind is capable. As we saw in the previous chapter, these are partly distinguished in terms of traditional subjects, but any new type of thinking which emerged could come to be considered part of one's educatedness, and to the extent that this exercised and developed our theoretical reason it could be redescribed in terms of self-realization, and to that extent seen as justified.

It might be objected here that the capacities for 'different forms of thought and awareness' correspond only to the knowledge *how* components of educatedness. It follows that, even if we grant that possession of this knowledge *how* is necessary to realize the theoretical reason fully, we have not thereby shown that any particular requirements in the sphere of knowledge *that* and knowledge *by acquaintance* are also necessary. In other words, it can be maintained that the intellectual self or theoretical reason can be realized in ways other than through educatedness as we have defined it. For example, someone might exercise and develop his theoretical reason by knowing one science or one period in history in great detail, whereas the educated man as we saw has a range of relevant knowledge in these fields. Again, a boy who knew all about the history and exploits of his favourite football team would thereby be exercising and developing his memory and perhaps also his historical capacity, but this particular kind of knowledge *that* is not included in educatedness. Or he might develop literary and philosophical skills through a study of *The Thoughts of Chairman Mao*, which is not part of the knowledge *by acquaintance* of the educated man in the way that the plays of Shakespeare are.

Now it should be pointed out here that none of these arguments precludes us from seeing educatedness as one form of intellectual self-realization; for what they would show is not that the educated man is not an intellectually self-realized man at all but only that he is not the only man who is intellectually self-realized. In other words, we have so far shown that educatedness, while it may be *sufficient* for intellectual self-realization, is not *necessary*. If it is sufficient – if the educated man is intellectually self-realized – we might still use the idea of intellectual self-realization as an attractive redescription of education. But unless we can show that intellectual self-realization demands a particular content to its knowledge, we cannot use the notion to defend education against other suggested forms of cultivation of the mind which have no fixed content – against the idea that, if the mind can be cultivated equally well by learning about governments and, say, footballers, it does not matter which is studied.

The next argument we shall consider fills this gap, and attempts to show that the particular knowledge *that* and knowledge *by acquaintance* requirements of education are also necessary conditions of intellectual self-realization. We shall argue for this thesis by suggesting that the requirements we laid down in Chapter Two for the knowledge *that* and knowledge *by acquaintance* of the educated man are also needed for intellectual self-realization, if this is to be seen as including the exercise as well as the development of intellectual capacities. Take, for example, the requirements of wide range and relevance in knowledge *that*. Even if we grant that the capacity to think historically or scientifically can be *developed* without acquiring the educated man's range of historical and scientific knowledge, the maximum *exercise* of these capacities in everyday life will depend on whether the person in question possesses the right pieces of knowledge *that* or not. And these pieces are precisely those which satisfy the education requirements of being wide-ranging and relevant. A similar argument could be produced concerning the relevance and range of knowledge of works of art: if the only literature a person knows is *The Thoughts of Chairman Mao*, he will not be able to bring it to bear on a very wide range of his life and culture. Similar considerations apply to the requirement of importance in the knowledge of the educated person, a requirement which is, as we saw, necessary for further understanding in the sphere in question: there are some objects of knowledge *that* and knowledge *by acquaintance* which have been the basis for so many succeeding writings and discoveries that the latter cannot be fully understood without an understanding of the former. This may be said to be true of the plays of Shakespeare: in the end it is for the pupil to decide whether he values for itself modern poetry as opposed to Shakespearian drama or whether he likes Graham Greene rather than Ian Fleming, but without knowledge of central works of literature such as Shakespearian drama a person will not have the necessary understanding to exercise his critical faculties and arrive at a rational evaluation. We can sum up this argument by saying that intellectual self-realization involves living the life of the 'thinking person' – and for that one needs education.

We conclude therefore that educatedness is not only a sufficient but also a necessary condition for the realization of the theoretical aspect of the self or of the distinctive human endowment.

It might be objected, however, that we have written as though the only thing of importance about a person's theoretical reason is that aspect of it which he has in common with all other persons. But in fact the theoretical reason, though part of the common 'distinctive endowment', manifests itself in particular ways in different individuals; and it might fairly be claimed that education is not sufficient for the realization of the theoretical aspect of the distinctive endowment unless it can cater for these individual differences. If it cannot, and if this degree of individuality is essential to the realization of theoretical reason, then the educated man is not after all a self-realized man, even in the theoretical sphere. Let us then investigate how far educatedness includes the realization of these individual aspects of the theoretical reason.

The first point to note is that there are *two* kinds of theoretical individuality (if we may use this term for short). The first kind is independent-mindedness: thinking for oneself, forming one's own judgments, etc. The second kind is idiosyncrasy of talent and inclination: each person has his own unique combination of intellectual gifts and leanings. Independent-mindedness concerns freedom from interference by others, whereas idiosyncrasy concerns differences from other people. These two features raise rather different issues for education, so we shall consider each separately, beginning with independent-mindedness.

At first it might seem that independent-mindedness, as such, is an extremely important part of what it is to be educated. Is not the educated man one who thinks for himself, whose judgments are his own and so on? This is perfectly true. But it is interesting to note that in a sense the mention of the independent-mindedness of the educated man is superfluous, since his independent-mindedness is not an extra feature separate from those attributes we have already assigned to him. In that he is critical as well as assimilative, he is independent-minded – one might express this point epigrammatically by saying that to think is to think for oneself.

But while educatedness is a sufficient condition of independent-mindedness, it is not a necessary one. It is clearly possible to think for oneself, in the sense of being critical of what one is told and insisting on making up one's own mind on issues rather than accepting second-hand opinions, without being educated in the sense in which we have been using the term. It follows that, while we can appeal to the concept of independent-mindedness as part of a redescription of educatedness, we cannot use it to *defend* educatedness as against other states of mind which include independent-mindedness. Moreover, not just any kind of independent-mindedness is aimed at in education. This may seem controversial in view of the common idea that anything which is 'original' is as such of educational value. But we wish to challenge this idea, so we must examine it briefly.

By 'original' here we mean 'springing from the pupil's own mind' rather than 'novel, fresh, creative': roughly speaking, the sense in which 'original' is opposed to 'derived' or 'copied', as distinct from that opposed to 'traditional, familiar'. Something can clearly be original in the first sense without being original in the second; for example, a philosophy student can think up, entirely by himself, an argument that is in fact a very familiar one. To examine the suggestion that originality in the first sense is an educational value, let us consider extreme cases. Quite often a teacher is offered a piece of work, described as 'original, anyway' or 'all my own ideas', which is not an example of the relevant kind of thinking at all: rhetoric instead of philosophy, or gossipy surmise instead of history, or personal anecdote instead of literary criticism. We submit that such things are of educational *dis*value, not because they are original but because they ignore the objective canons of appropriateness governing the form of thought in question. Hence originality cannot be a good thing as such – at least, unless one is to say that anyone's personal outpourings are a good thing.

Of course this is an extreme case. A more attractive possibility is that of the original essay which is clearly philosophy, history or whatever, but because no other works have been consulted is full of basic confusions, ignores vital data and so on. Here we might allow a value to the originality, saying 'At least he tries to work it out for himself' – but the value is not really in his independence of *other people*, but rather in the fact that he is really *doing* philosophy or history, rather than merely reporting on the doing of it by others. We might wish to add that if the pupil's aim is really to do history or philosophy, and not simply to 'be original', he must take due note of the work of others as this is the only way to achieve his aim.

It may be retorted here that if a piece of work is *completely* derivative it has no educational value, and hence originality *must* be required. But in fact the premise is not obviously true. If a student copies something out of a book or lectures, he is certainly not himself *doing* philosophy or history or literary criticism but he may be learning something for all that, and so his work may have more value than the 'original' work which we first described. Of course, the question of the *moral* value of the two works – whether they indicate laziness or conceit or cowardice, for example – is another question altogether, though it bedevils discussion of this topic.

We conclude then that while independent-mindedness of the right kind (not just any form of 'originality') is an essential part of educatedness, educatedness is not a necessary condition of independent-mindedness, and therefore the degree to which the latter concept can be used in justification by redescription is limited.

We turn now to the other kind of individuality shown within the human endowment of theoretical reason: that of idiosyncratic talents. Here it might plausibly be maintained that the demands of education are actually incompatible with the fullest realization of idiosyncratic talents. Not only do they stress the intellectual aspects of personality, regardless of whether a particular person is intellectually gifted; they also require, even within the intellectual sphere, a breadth of interest which is not natural to most people.

It might be objected that this is only part of the story. It seems to fit best the educational stages which are covered in the earlier years at school, where a good deal of stress is laid on the idea of *general* education, and the assumption is that everyone is capable of this. As a child gets older, however, he is quite often allowed, or even encouraged, to 'drop' those subjects for which he has little aptitude and/or inclination. It follows (the objector asserts) that education does after all cater for idiosyncratic talent.

But we can reply that dropping subjects simply because one lacks aptitude for them is imposed not by educational values but by practical possibilities. If a person is incapable of developing more than a certain degree in some directions (and this is in varying degrees true of everyone) the only kind of education *possible* for him is one which reflects his individual aptitudes to some extent, and hence perforce embodies some measure of idiosyncratic self-realization. But this, so far from being educationally valuable, is often held to be detrimental to education if it goes too far. Indeed, an over-lopsided curriculum cannot count as educative at all, because it robs the pupils of the breadth which is by definition part of education, and a pupil who is capable only of such a curriculum, because he possesses a sufficiently serious 'blind spot', can never become truly educated.

Do the same points apply in the context of sixth form and higher education, where at first sight individual talent might seem more important? To some extent they do, insofar as practical possibilities rather than educational values again govern the degree to which individuality of talent is developed: if it is the case that only certain people are capable, in terms of their natural talents, of profiting by higher education, then higher education must for them be a measure of idiosyncratic self-realization, for purely practical reasons. It may be pointed out, however, that in justifying higher education to someone, we often make use of considerations of individuality of talent as a positive value, not merely a practical limitation: 'You've got this brain that not everyone has – you should develop it, it's your gift, your talent', etc. This is true, but it should be noted that apart from this very broad conception, of the talent which not everyone has, the aims of higher education do not incorporate the realization of individual theoretical talent. This is not at first obvious, because of the stress laid within higher education on specialization. But this is not for the sake of catering for different talents, and may even conflict with it. For whereas early education forces even the lopsided person to be general, higher education forces even the versatile person to specialize, at least in some measure. This fact shows that the point of it is not primarily to cater for individual differences of aptitude but to reach a level of understanding, which is impossible if the net is cast too widely. It may incidentally cater for idiosyncratic self-realization in the case of a person who is good only at one or two subjects, but this is the exception rather than the rule among people who are capable of higher education at all.

We conclude then that education cannot in general be redescribed or justified in terms of idiosyncratic self-realization. It is trivially true, at one level, that education takes account of individual differences (it could not go on otherwise); at other levels it is false. This conclusion, taken together with our conclusions about independent-mindedness, suggests that educatedness cannot convincingly be defended by appeal to the *individual* aspects of theoretical self-realization; any such defence must concentrate on the realization of theoretical reason seen as a feature which is alike in every person. How far this limitation is considered a serious one depends on how much stress one wishes to lay on the individual aspects of the theoretical reason.

Let us assume then that, subject to this limitation, we can justify educatedness in that we can redescribe it as the realization of the intellectual self. It might nevertheless be pointed out that, according to our earlier account, there is much more to a person than the exercise and development of his theoretical reason: there are the two aspects of his practical reason – the self-determining and rule-following aspects – and there is his emotional life. How far can they be realized by education?

It must by now be clear that we do not expect that on our account of the educated man the whole nature of a person can be realized through education. We are adopting a narrow view of what it is to be educated, and therefore if it emerges, as it will, that education cannot bring about the realization of all aspects of the self our withers remain unwrung, for on our view education is not of the whole man. Nevertheless, it may be of more of the man than we have so far been able to bring out in our account of the realization of the intellectual aspects of the person. If this proves to be the case it is useful in the defence of education against its detractors. For one possible line of attack on education in our sense has always been that it caters for only one aspect of the personality and ignores or even impairs other more important aspects. If we show that this is not true to the degree supposed, we have weakened this attack on education.

One important aspect of personality is the ability to be self-determining, or to make choices which are peculiarly one's own. It might fairly be claimed that the exercise and development of this ability are essential to the realization of one's nature as a person. How far does education realize this side to the life of a person?

It might be thought that we have already dealt with this question, under the heading of independent-mindedness. But independent-mindedness belongs to the theoretical reason, whereas the quality we are now considering belongs to the practical reason: it concerns not thinking for oneself, but choosing and acting for oneself. Can the educated man be redescribed as self-determining in this sense? It seems fairly clear that he cannot. Presumably the reasoning which he employs in deliberating about courses of action will (other things being equal) be critical and cogent, characteristic of an educated man. But initiative, determination, decisiveness and so on – the qualities which make up self-determination – are not part of the definition of educatedness. These are qualities of motivation which the educated man may or may not possess. This is not to say that motivation is entirely outside the sphere of educatedness. As we saw in the previous chapter, the cultivation of certain inclinations, such as curiosity and critical spirit, are built into it, and it may follow that within the scope of *these* motives the educated man is likely to be reasonably self-determined: for example, he may tend to be enterprising about research plans, tenacious in carrying them out, not readily deflected by others' attacks, and so on. (We said 'may', because in fact it seems logically quite possible for a person whom in other ways one would wish to call highly educated to lack self-determination even in this sphere, because he lacks more general qualities of will.) But outside the sphere of intellectual activity the educated man is logically no more likely than any other to stick to his guns, form his own plans and so forth. Of course modern educational methods, with their emphasis on carrying out projects, aim to cultivate pupils' self-determination among other things. But this aim need not be seen as an educational one. It is part of character-building, a complementary aim which schools go in for alongside their educational aims.

Having considered the extent to which the educated man might be regarded as being self-realized with respect to his capacity for self-determination, let us proceed to say something about the extent to which education realizes the capacity to be rule-following and to experience emotion. The capacity to be rule-following is mainly exercised and developed in the moral life, and we shall say quite a lot about this when we discuss moral education in our next chapter. Briefly, our conclusions will be that whereas the educated man is necessarily well-equipped to *know* what he ought to do, he is no better able to do it than the less well-educated – a conclusion parallel to that about self-determination. Hence educatedness cannot be described as realizing human nature in its rule-following capacity.

The capacity for emotion is exercised and developed through the aesthetic aspects of education. We said that the capacity to experience emotion in a characteristically human way involves reason, and the development of this capacity is brought about by the study of art which is part of educatedness. There are decided limitations, however, to the extent to which education leads to the realization of this capacity. The educated man has finely discriminated emotions, but human beings also have the capacity for feeling *strong* emotion and the capacity for displaying uninhibited physical energy and strength. Both these kinds of capacity (what we may call, without intending to derogate, 'animal' capacities) can either be exercised or left latent, and presumably also developed or allowed to atrophy. The capacity for strength of emotion is especially significant here, as it is widely believed that this capacity is not merely ignored but actually impaired by the development of the more intellectual capacities of theoretical reason. In other words, the process of education, far from leading to the realization of this aspect of a person, is likely to run counter to it.

We conclude this attempt to justify educatedness, redescribed in terms of the realization of the self, by noting that the attempt is successful only within certain very narrow limits. Educatedness can be redescribed in terms of the realization of the theoretical reason, or what we have called the 'intellectual self', insofar as this is not seen in individual terms. To a limited extent educatedness can be redescribed in terms of the realization of the capacity for feeling emotions. But this falls far short of the realization of all the capacities of a person. A person can be described as highly educated who is at the same time hopelessly bad at personal relations, incapable of planning his life, morally underdeveloped and lacking the capacity for strong feelings or physical strength. This limitation might not matter from the justificatory point of view if we could maintain that, while educatedness constituted the realization of the theoretical reason, other aspects of the self could be realized alongside it. But in fact too much education is often thought to be one cause of *deficiencies* in these other spheres, and if such a belief has any foundation, the appeal to self-realization becomes a rather two-edged weapon in the hand of the would-be justifier of education. For in terms of self-realization, educatedness can be shown to be a good in itself, but very much only one good, to be weighed up against other goods which may not be entirely compatible with it.

4 Conclusion

In this chapter we have examined some of the arguments which seek to justify education, not in terms of its good consequences, but as a good in itself. We considered first the transcendental argument of R. S. Peters, which aimed to show that the pursuit of intellectual activities is in effect presupposed in asking for a justification of them. We came to the conclusion that the extent to which this is so is far too slight to cover the scope of education and that in any case it does not furnish a justification of the activities. We next examined the intuition that the state of educatedness is simply good in itself, pointing out that such a position is of its very nature not susceptible to proof, and endeavouring to meet some of the difficulties inherent in such a position. Finally we turned to what we called the re-description form of argument, whereby a thing is justified if it can be seen as an example of or equivalent to something already acknowledged to be good in itself. We considered a redescription of educatedness in terms of self-realization, and concluded that such a redescription offered only a very limited justification. For while educatedness can be adequately described as the realization of the theoretical reason, it does not involve the realization of some other important aspects of the self.

Chapter Four

Justifications: extrinsic aims

We have considered attempts to justify education in terms of its intrinsic ends or aims – attempts to show that it is worthwhile in itself. We shall now examine a number of arguments which have this in common, that they attempt to justify education in terms of various goods which it is thought can be brought about by education. These goods are of three different although overlapping types: those concerning the individual himself (his own good, pleasure, interest, happiness, etc.), those concerning morality or other phenomena generally assumed to be morally good, such as friendship or religion, and those concerning the good of society. The fact that goods of these types overlap does not make clear discussion easy. Moreover, confusion is multiplied by the fact that the same concepts can occur, in a different logical form, in redescription arguments of the kind we discussed when we considered justifications of education in terms of its intrinsic ends. For example, the concept of 'interest' might occur in a redescription argument if we maintain that educatedness is a part of someone's interests in the sense of his good. Again, there is a sense of 'happiness' which could occur in a redescription argument, and conversely the redescription argument in terms of the concept of self-realization which we in fact discussed in Chapter Three could be restated as an attempted justification in terms of an extrinsic end of education, if we said that education *leads* to self-realization. We shall try to avoid these confusions at each stage by drawing attention to the different directions in which the argument might turn. Before we develop the first attempt to justify education in terms of its extrinsic ends, however, it might be helpful to discuss what would *count* as a justification of this sort.

1 *Types of extrinsic justification*

There are stronger and weaker senses in which X might be said to be justified in that it brought about Y. In the strongest sense of justification the occurrence of X is both a necessary and a sufficient causal condition of Y, where Y is taken to be some good. In a weaker sense, X is simply a necessary causal condition of Y – it has to take place in order for Y to happen, but it is not sufficient by itself for the occurrence of Y. In a still weaker sense, X may be conducive to Y – it may make Y more likely, for example, or it may be necessary for the best forms of Y. We shall find that the strongest form of justification does not apply to education in relation to the various extrinsic ends we shall discuss. But this in itself need not worry us; if education is necessary for, or conducive to, a sufficient number of important things, it is surely extrinsically justified.

It might be objected that there is a fourth sense of justification which is logically possible and here relevant – that in which X is a sufficient, but not a necessary, condition for the occurrence of Y. For example, it might be said that a visit to the seaside would be a sufficient but not a necessary condition of an enjoyable holiday. Does this give us a relevant sort of justification? It does if all that is at stake is doing X or not doing X. Suppose, however, we are faced with alternatives which are themselves open to assessment and choice in terms of various sets of criteria. In that event the claim that X was a sufficient causal condition of Y would not *by itself* give us a justification for doing X; we would also need to know whether X satisfied the other relevant sets of criteria. And this is certainly something we would need to know in the case of education, since it is arduous, time-consuming and expensive, and therefore would tend not to be highly rated in terms of many types of criteria for choice. Suppose, for instance, that we could show that education was a sufficient causal condition of individual happiness, but we could also show that a life of luxury and ease was a sufficient causal condition of happiness. Faced with this alternative method of attaining happiness, which is easier and no doubt cheaper, we can hardly justify the pursuit of education by referring to happiness. For this reason we shall mean by 'justified' either 'conducive to a good' or 'a necessary condition of a good' or 'a necessary and a sufficient condition of a good'.

Before we discuss the possibilities of justifications of these kinds, perhaps we should make clear that these causal conditions are different in kind from the *logically* necessary and sufficient conditions of the previous chapter. X is a *causal* condition of Y if it is necessary or sufficient for the occurrence of Y; by contrast, X is a *logical* condition of Y if a thing's being X is logically necessary or sufficient for its being describable as Y also. Thus education would be a causal condition of wealth, if it brings wealth about, but a logical condition of culture, if to be educated logically implies that one can be described also as cultured. But, as we saw just now, the distinction between one thing's resulting from another and one thing's being describable in terms of another is not always a sharp one.

2 *Education and its consequences for the individual*

Under this heading we propose to consider a number of closely connected concepts which occur in arguments intended to show that through being educated a person can obtain various goods for himself, or satisfy his wants in ways he otherwise could not. These concepts overlap to such an extent that it is not possible to discuss one without the others, although in fact similar considerations arise for them all. Let us take first the concept of pleasure as it provides as good a way as any into this particular jungle, and it also illustrates the confusing manner in which the concepts in this group interact and presuppose each other.

The term 'pleasure' is very complex in its use. For one thing it can be used both for a reaction to something (to use a vague non-question-begging word for the moment) and for the object of that reaction. In the first sense a person may say, 'Reading *gives* me a lot of pleasure', or, 'I get much pleasure *from* reading'; he may convey the same thing employing the second sense if he says, 'Reading *is* one of my pleasures'. A further complication is that the word 'pleasure', whether in the 'reaction' sense or the 'source of reaction' sense, covers both enjoyment and being pleased at, with or by. These seem however to be two different phenomena, at any rate in terms of the kind of source from which they arise. I can logically be pleased at anything which it makes sense for me to want, whereas I can logically enjoy only my own activities and experiences. Apparent counter-examples can all be redescribed in such a way as to meet these criteria. Thus it may be objected that *I* can enjoy *your* success. But note that this does not mean the same as being pleased by your success; it means enjoying some experience which your success brings *me*, such as basking in reflected glory or watching your own elation. Again, it may be objected that one can enjoy *things*: a meal, a book. But this always means either that one enjoyed the activity of eating the meal or reading the book, or that the 'thing' is itself an experience or bundle of experiences: parties or holidays.

Does the difference between enjoying and being pleased go beyond a difference in the sources from which they arise? They certainly seem to have different relationships to wishes and desires. To enjoy something, I need not have wanted it beforehand – unexpected enjoyment is very common – but while I am enjoying it, it is analytic that I want it to continue, or to recur, or at least not to be interrupted, depending on the type of thing enjoyed. It is in fact a species of interest, in the 'being interested in' sense, marked off from other cases by being unforced and reasonably direct – concerned with the nature of the object in itself, rather than with the consequences or wider aspects of it. To be pleased with something, on the other hand, suggests previous wants – not necessarily for the thing itself, but for other things to which it is conducive or which it exemplifies. Thus, if I am pleased by your engagement, this means that I wanted either this in particular, or something which embraces it, such as your happiness, or something which it brings me, such as a relief from the strain of your unsuccessful affairs. Let us now consider how these two kinds of pleasure relate to education, taking firstly enjoyment.

There could be many ways of justifying education in terms of enjoyment. Before we can consider them, however, we must dispose of the argument that, since strictly speaking our reason for aiming at something cannot be that it produces enjoyment, it is logically impossible to justify education in terms of the enjoyment it brings. But why should it be held that a reason for aiming at something cannot be 'because it produces enjoyment'? The answer is that some philosophers claim that to do something for the sake of enjoyment or pleasure is really equivalent to doing it for its own sake, so that no additional information is given as to why it is done by speaking of enjoyment or pleasure as though they were a separable result. For example, to say, 'I play golf because I enjoy it', is claimed to be just another way of saying, 'I play golf just for its own sake'. This claim has some point in it, for, as we saw, enjoyment is a reaction to an activity's empirical nature, a reaction which does not appeal to more remote considerations such as duty or usefulness. On the other hand, to do something for the sake of enjoyment is not simply equivalent to doing it for the sake of doing it; indeed, a person can do something for its own sake while admitting that he does not enjoy doing it. To do something for the sake of enjoyment is to do it because it produces a result, namely a certain reaction in the *doer*, such that if the reaction did not occur he would cease doing it. It is therefore informative to say that someone does something for the sake of enjoyment.

We can therefore return to the claims that a person's aim in undergoing education, and others' aim in subjecting him to it, is to produce enjoyment; and that this aim can provide a justification of education. As we said earlier, this justification could arise in various ways: thus it could be claimed that the process of education is itself enjoyable, that the worthwhile activities into which it initiates us are enjoyable, and that education enables us to 'enjoy life', as we say. (The latter two are the most important here; the claim that the *process* is enjoyable is usually used as a defence against attacks rather than as a justification in itself.) But it could quite well be objected that even if the factual claims be true, that the worthwhile activities are enjoyable and that the educated man's life is enjoyable, these do not constitute a justification. Thus, it might be held either that enjoyment has no independent value but takes its value, good or bad, from its source – this would be Aristotle's view, for example[1] – or that while enjoyment as such is a good, there is no reason to suppose that education brings *more* enjoyment than lack of education.

We shall not discuss the Aristotelian position at length here since it involves too many complexities, similar to those which arise for Mill's qualitative distinction of pleasures.[2] It is sufficient for our purposes to say that on this view of enjoyment one clearly cannot appeal to it as a justification of that which is enjoyed, but only *vice versa*. But the second view (which need not involve the Benthamite assumption that pleasure is the *only* good) at least allows that enjoyment is a good. This notion of enjoyment would enable us to produce a justification for education, if we could make out that the educated man has in fact more enjoyment than the uneducated man.

This claim is sometimes treated as though it were obviously true, but in fact it is by no means obvious. Consider first the common appeal to the superiority, in quantity of enjoyment produced, of intellectual and aesthetic activities. Now it may be the case that the educated man enjoys reading more than he enjoys the pleasures which are alleged to be characteristic of the uneducated man, such as eating. Even this is doubtful in many cases (unless it is made true by definition, along the lines of Aldous Huxley's 'An intellectual is a man who has found something which interests him more than sex'). But even if it were true, it is not relevant. The relevant comparison is with the amount of enjoyment he would have had if uneducated, and there is no way of knowing how the two lives compare.

Various commonsense empirical points can, however, be made in favour of the thesis that the educated man is capable of more enjoyment. We may suggest that since any given enjoyment tends to pall after a time, it is an advantage to be able to enjoy a large

[1] Aristotle, *Nicomachean Ethics*, 1175b20.
[2] J. S. Mill, *Utilitarianism*, ch. II, pp. 258–62 (London, Collins, The Fontana Library, 1962).

variety of different things; this the educated man can do, since he can appreciate intellectual and aesthetic pleasures as well as other kinds. Furthermore, the less demanding an enjoyed activity is, the more quickly it palls; so intellectual and aesthetic activities, being demanding pursuits, have the advantage that they can be indulged in with pleasure for a comparatively large proportion of one's time.[1]

But these points rest on the assumption that the educated man in question is able to pursue the intellectual life, at least in some measure. And in a particular case this may not be possible. The traditional defences (e.g. by Plato and Aristotle) of the pleasures of the intellect assume that the philosopher or contemplative has achieved *leisure*. But this is not possible for all educated men nowadays, and even where it is they might hold it their duty to go back to the cave, in Plato's phrase.[2] At this point it may be objected that we have ignored the other aspect of the claim that the educated man gets more enjoyment: that education enables a man to enjoy life in general more, whatever specific activities he may find himself engaged in. But this too is a rather controversial claim. It is true that the educated man will enjoy many things lost on the uneducated man. For example, he may enjoy his walk to work because of the interest he finds in the differing styles of the buildings he passes. But there will also be many things which he will *not* enjoy which the uneducated person would: for example, he may find a lively discussion in the office merely irritating, because so many questions are begged and terms undefined; or he may find the office reproductions of popular art tasteless and sentimental.

We conclude therefore that one cannot justify educating someone on the grounds that this will bring him more enjoyment, because whether it does or not is very much a contingent matter, depending on his particular circumstances. Education is therefore neither a necessary nor a sufficient condition of enjoyment. Of course, it does not follow that a person would not prefer to be educated rather than not, notwithstanding these considerations. A person can choose something for reasons which have nothing to do with enjoyment.

[1] R. S. Peters, *Ethics and Education*, pp. 155–6, 157–8 (London, Allen and Unwin, 1966).

[2] Plato, *Republic*, 514A–520E, esp. 519D.

For example, he might think that education is worthwhile in some other way. Or he might think that it would bring him pleasure in the 'being pleased' sense, or again, bring him happiness. To consideration of these latter ideas we must now turn.

It is not at first clear how a justification of education can be furnished in terms of pleasure in the other sense, viz. being pleased at, with or by. For it hardly seems informative as a justification to say 'I educated him because I thought he would be pleased to be educated'. What is wrong with this is that being pleased is, as we saw, logically dependent on the existence of *wants*, either for the object of the pleasure or for something connected with it. To say that a person is being educated because he would be pleased with the result is really to say that it was done because of some want he has, either for education as such or for something which it exemplifies or promotes; in other words, that education either forms part of, or is in, his *interest*. (Note that we are using 'interest' here to refer to his actual wants, not in the other sense of 'good, well-being or welfare', which may or may not be the same thing.)

Now the question whether a person's wants, as such, constitute a *justification* of his trying to get something (or others' trying to get it for him), as distinct from merely an *explanation*, is of course a controversial one. By this we mean, not that other people's wants may conflict with his, but that the question whether his wants constitute even a *prima facie* justification can be raised, on the grounds that what he wants may not be good at all, and, if it is, the justification resides in the goodness, not in his wanting it. We shall not attempt to settle this question here, but simply point out that even if the broadly utilitarian position is adopted, that a person should have what he wants (subject to others' wants), we can justify education thereby only in some cases. These will be the cases where a person wants to be educated either for itself or for what it brings.

It may be objected that education must be in everyone's interests, in that a man who is educated can so much more easily get whatever he wants. But this is not necessarily the case. It is true that a person with educational *qualifications* can often earn more money and this is useful for many different purposes. But this justifies only trying to acquire the qualifications as such – at the expense of one's education if need be – and in any case it is a highly contingent matter whether those with high qualifications do earn more. It may also be true that an educated person 'knows his way around' – can understand instructions, work out his tax allowances, follow a map and so on. But these points apply also to a person who is not really educated beyond a certain point, but who has picked up certain skills; and from the point of view of 'knowing one's way around' it would clearly be better to concentrate school and university time on just such practical matters, and leave out much of what we consider essential to education.

Of course, it may also be said that education is itself part of everyone's interests – that everyone wants to be educated as such. But this is not very plausible either. It may be the case, as Mill thought, that all human beings have a sense of dignity.[1] But many people would not see being educated as required by their dignity at all, and indeed it would be perfectly possible to hold that one's dignity required its absence. We conclude then that neither enjoyment nor being pleased furnish a general and unambiguous justification of education, in that education is neither necessary nor sufficient for their existence.

Many of the same points arise with regard to happiness. But, like 'pleasure', 'happiness' is an ambiguous word. We can distinguish a psychological sense – that which is sometimes called the 'hedonistic' conception – and the evaluative, 'eudaemonistic' sense. The hedonistic sense is that connected with people's actual wishes, and means something like 'satisfaction of major goals, together with absence of major frustrations' or 'being pleased with life as a whole'. It is obviously connected with pleasure, in the 'being pleased' rather than the enjoyment sense (except insofar as enjoying himself is a major goal for a particular person). Whether or not education brings happiness in this sense is very much a contingent matter, depending on what a person's actual wants are. As we have just seen, there is no reason to suppose either that education itself is among everyone's wants or that it always brings people what they want. Hence, given the above definition of happiness, there is no reason to suppose that education is necessarily conducive to happiness.

[1] Mill, op. cit., ch. II, p. 260.

The eudaemonistic sense of happiness is roughly equivalent to 'truly fortunate' or 'truly enviable'. It is in this sense that a Victorian father says 'unhappy girl' to his fallen daughter, meaning not that she has got what she does not want but that she is to be pitied by anyone of sound view. It is this conception of happiness which Aristotle employs in his *Ethics* and equates with the good for man; it is equivalent to the second sense of 'interest' mentioned above, namely 'good, well-being, welfare'. The question of how far this second conception of happiness can be used in a justification of education is clearly a complex one. Insofar as the justification is in terms of *extrinsic* ends, it seems to depend on the various conclusions reached in the course of this chapter. For the ingredients of a man's good or welfare in this sense are presumably such things as his moral character, his personal relationships, his enjoyment of life, his material prosperity; and the problem of whether or how far education is conducive to these things is precisely what this chapter tries to solve. But education might be seen not as a means to its possessor's welfare but as itself constituting one part of that welfare, and justified on that account. This sort of justification, however, is not one in terms of extrinsic ends. It is really a justification by redescription of the kind we discussed in Chapter Three: educatedness is claimed to be worthwhile because it can be described as part of the good for man, which is (it is supposed) agreed to be worthwhile. In that case we can deal with it along the lines of the discussion of self-realization: perhaps educatedness can be described as man's intellectual good, but, as we saw, this is only one aspect of man.

Before we conclude this section perhaps we might mention a difficulty which applies to all aspects of it, but in two different ways. People sometimes hold that they have a *duty* to seek education or more education for themselves. But it might be argued that if they are right this fact renders irrelevant the whole argument of this section, on the grounds that we have construed education as justified in terms of the possessor's benefit, and one cannot (logically) have a duty to oneself.[1] This objection, however, seems to have rather a different force according to whether it is concerned with the

[1] See R. S. Downie and Elizabeth Telfer, *Respect For Persons*, pp. 76–81 (London, Allen and Unwin, 1969).

individual's good or his *eudaemonia* on the one hand, or his enjoyment, wants and (hedonistic) happiness on the other. There is no reason why one should not have a duty to oneself with regard to the former, and we would wish to argue for this. The question of duties to seek the latter is more controversial – but perhaps if enjoyment, fulfilment of wishes and happiness are good in themselves (as we are often told) we *do* have a duty to seek them in all contexts – and hence for ourselves no less than for others. An argument to show this was *not* so would need to establish, either that there is a basic moral asymmetry between our own case and that of others,[1] or that we always tend to seek these things for ourselves anyway – so that talk of a duty to do so is pointless – and either of these claims needs a good deal of support.

The real difficulty in the attempt to justify the pursuit of education by saying that one of its extrinsic ends is the production of good consequences of one sort or another for the individual himself is quite a simple one: it is not at all clear that education beyond a minimum point is either necessary for or even conducive to these good consequences.

Let us now try to justify it by arguing that it produces moral goodness, and that whatever produces moral goodness is justifiable.

3 Education and moral goodness

Before we can discuss this topic in any detail we must distinguish two theses about it. One is that there is such a thing as moral education, which is part of education at large and which is conducive to (or perhaps necessary for) moral goodness. The other is that education as a *whole* is conducive to (or perhaps, again, necessary for) moral goodness. We shall examine each in turn, but it should be noted that it is the second thesis which is the more important for our purposes, for it is the one which is concerned with education as a whole and it is that, rather than *moral* education specifically, which we are attempting to justify. We are, however, including some dis-

---

[1] For a discussion of this idea, see W. G. Maclagan, 'Self and Others: A Defence of Altruism', *Philosophical Quarterly*, 1954.

cussion of the first thesis, partly because moral education is an aspect of education, and partly because moral education is important in its own right.

Before we can consider the first thesis we must give an account of moral education, which so far we have mentioned only in passing. We suggested in that account that moral education could be compared in some ways with the learning of aesthetic appreciation: to be educated in this sphere is not a question of possessing a series of 'correct' views, but rather of coming to hold a set of moral views which one can rationally defend. There is of course no reason why these should not be entirely similar to most conventional moral codes; what makes them characteristic of the morally educated person is not their content but the way in which they are espoused.

The phrase 'coming to hold a set of moral views' does, however, need some elucidation, for it blurs over a whole process of development. Consider first the word 'moral'. If a person is to be morally educated, he must grasp the particular idea which lies behind this word and which marks off the sphere of the moral from other spheres. As P. H. Hirst and R. S. Peters say, 'Moral judgment and awareness necessitate . . . another family of concepts such as "ought", "wrong" and "duty". Unless actions or states are understood in such terms, it is not their moral character of which we are aware.'[1] This is on the right lines, but one might wish to add '*morally* wrong', etc., since words such as 'ought' and 'wrong' occur in other spheres as well. What marks off the moral sphere from others is of course a matter of controversy. But we can to some extent say what morality is *not*; thus a child who thinks that what he ought to do simply means what will please his mother, or what he will be punished for omitting to do, or what will bring him satisfaction has not yet grasped the *moral* 'ought'. (There might, however, be disagreement as to whether or not someone who saw morality as the articulation of social principles necessary for living together with others had grasped the whole of the concept; could there not be other non-social moral 'oughts', and could there not be

[1] P. H. Hirst and R. S. Peters, *The Logic of Education*, pp. 63–4 (London, Routledge and Kegan Paul, The Students Library of Education, 1970).

a prior moral 'ought' presupposed, namely that we ought to live together?)

Let us assume, however, that there is a distinctively moral 'point of view', to understand which is indisputably part of educatedness. We would teach people about it because of its distinctiveness, even if we did not care about morality, just as the educated agnostic feels his children should learn about religious belief because it is 'part of our culture'. Part of this moral point of view is its rationality – to explain the moral point of view is to explain that moral 'oughts' are backed up by reasons, referring to other moral 'oughts', to the circumstances of the action, and so on. But of course this explanation is not done in a vacuum. In practice children possess already a moral or quasi-moral code and come across others, and the method therefore is to consider how and how far these can be defended; or they make or come across moral judgments, which can be examined in the light of various considerations, and so on.

So far we have written as though the aim of the educator in this sphere is a purely theoretical one, akin to that of the religious studies teacher talking in a detached manner about various religions. But in practice of course his aim is not only theoretical but also practical; he wishes his pupils not only to understand morality but to act morally. In order to do this they must themselves make moral judgments, not merely understand them. This process is a rather puzzling one. R. M. Hare talks as though it were entirely voluntary,[1] but it seems nearer the truth to say that, whereas the effort of weighing up pros and cons is a voluntary activity, the conclusion emerges on one side or the other whether we like it or not, carrying with it an attraction towards the type of action approved of or a repulsion from the type of action condemned which, however, falls short of actual decision to act accordingly.[2] A teacher who tells his pupils they ought to make up their minds on some moral issue is therefore telling them either to think about it until a conclusion emerges or to form a resolution to act in accordance with their convictions. Now that we have described the process of moral education let us consider the view that moral education is conducive to, or

[1] R. M. Hare, *Freedom and Reason*, pp. 1–6 (Oxford University Press, 1963).
[2] See R. S. Downie and Elizabeth Telfer, 'Autonomy', *Philosophy*, 1971.

even necessary for, moral goodness – the first of the theses propounded at the beginning of this section.

It might well be objected at the outset of the discussion that all this moral education is certainly not *necessary* for acting morally. A child can perfectly well do the right thing if he simply does what he has been brought up to do, without relating it to underlying principles or submitting it to questioning. This contention can be met firstly by reiterating the uniqueness of *moral* judgment; a child may be in a sense 'doing the right thing' if he simply does what his parents say, but if this is just to please them it is not *moral* action at all. Secondly we may query whether someone who does not examine his moral views is as likely to do the right thing in all circumstances as someone who does. He may coast along happily in conventional situations, but will lack the apparatus to make a reasonable decision in a more unusual case. (We can maintain this without assuming that morality is objective; it applies on any view of this latter question, provided a distinction between 'more' and 'less' reasonable is possible in terms of it.) This second argument shows that moral education is *conducive* to morality, in the following sense: while not necessary for all moral situations, it is necessary for the realization of the highest possibilities of moral character, those in which a person behaves well in every kind of situation.

The contender may provide two counter-arguments. The first is that so long as a person does what *he* thinks is right he is not to blame[1] – so long as he 'means well', therefore, his moral stature cannot be raised by moral education. But this is confused: he can be doing the wrong thing even if he cannot be blamed for it, and in any case he *is* blameworthy if he has neglected his moral education and is led into false judgment as a result. The second counter-argument is that moral education, far from being necessary, is a positive hazard, because all this questioning of moral judgments may itself lead people astray. If this means that moral education sometimes leads people to throw over precepts which they were brought up on but now sincerely and with reasons hold to be mistaken, the counter-argument has no case: perhaps the new generation are right on the issue. But if it means that moral education gives people better

[1] See Downie and Telfer, op. cit., pp. 300–301.

tools for sophistry, cynicism and successful self-deception there *is* a case against moral education, albeit not a conclusive one: to be morally highly educated doubtless makes a person open to kinds of temptation that the morally less educated avoid, as well as capable of heights which they cannot reach.

Before we leave the first thesis we must deal with a difficulty which besets the concept of moral education: namely, that the teacher has no status as a moral expert, in the way he has in his particular subject, and therefore has no right to carry on moral education. Now this objection to some extent begs one of the questions we are discussing, namely whether the educated person has, in virtue of his education, a truer view of morality than the uneducated person; for presumably the teacher is to be regarded as an educated person, and his pupils (and some of their parents) as less so. But in any case he need not (and in most cases will not) claim any special status in order to carry on moral education. He will simply be a kind of chairman of the discussion. If he attempts to lay down dogmatic positions which his pupils have not the equipment to challenge his activity is counter-educational, because it discourages the kind of thinking and questioning which he should be trying to promote. Of course there may be a place for him to declare his own convictions on an issue and explain how they might be defended, particularly perhaps if they are unconventional; but then he is acting simply as one participant in a debate, and is educating by showing the possibility of another point of view, not by imposing *his* view as the correct one. Problems of course arise if he thereby convinces his pupils that some type of conduct which their parents would condemn is permissible. But if he has led them to think for *themselves* (where they are of an age to do so) and not merely indoctrinated them, can he be faulted? The conclusion of our discussion of the first thesis, then, is that moral education is conducive to moral goodness, in the sense described above. As we said to begin with, however, this conclusion does not justify education as a whole. Let us therefore turn to the second thesis mentioned at the beginning of the section: the view that education in general is conducive to moral goodness.

It may be argued that the distinction between this thesis and the first is an unreal one, on the grounds that moral education as we have described it is not a separate item on the curriculum, but is carried on in the course of other teaching and in the course of school life in general. Thus a teacher of English or history may well discuss his pupils' moral views as to the conduct of fictional or historical characters, and in so doing be drawn into a more general discussion, pointing out the relevance of factors they had not considered to cases of a certain kind, and so on. Or he may take the opportunity of some misdemeanour to explain why such conduct is disapproved of, compare it with cases the children would grasp more readily, etc.

Now it may be granted that there is not (as a rule) a separate subject called 'moral education'. But it does not follow from this that moral education cannot be distinguished from education as a whole. For the concepts which belong to morality can quite well be grasped by someone who knows nothing about literature or history. These subjects may be useful vehicles for moral education, but it is not clear that they are essential – indeed a person might learn better from 'life' than in the context of academic subjects, especially if there is a thoughtful person at hand to teach him.

Having reiterated that general education *is* distinguishable from moral education as such, we can begin to defend the second thesis. Our suggestion is that education in general is conducive to moral goodness because it helps people to acquire the *non*-moral knowledge which is sometimes necessary for a sound moral judgment. Consider for example a headmaster who is trying to decide whether he has a moral duty to allow Pakistani girl pupils to wear Moslem dress in school. To make a sound judgment on this issue he needs to know not only about the relevant moral factors, such as: it is wrong to cause unnecessary distress, it is wrong to be partial to one group, it is wrong to interfere with people's religions, it is wrong to encourage unhygienic clothes, it is wrong to destroy a distinct culture, it is wrong to emphasize cultural differences where tensions in any case exist. He also needs to know some of the non-moral facts: about the place of such clothes in the religion, about the likely feelings of the participants (might the elders be mollified eventually? might the adolescents be ostracized?), about the effects of such clothes on hygiene, about the likely social effects. These facts are not moral facts, but the kind of things learnt in history or biology or social science; and the educated person is equipped to find out answers to such questions – to distinguish attested medical fact from prejudice, for example. Literature and history have their place here too, as ways of learning how people are apt to feel and react in certain situations – though some would say real-life experience is the best teacher here.

But the relevance of general education to sound moral judgment is not simply that it enables a person to acquire the non-moral information that he needs: the critical disposition which the educated person develops is important in this context, as it will prompt him to reject some forms of spurious moral argument. But, as we saw before, this disposition is not necessarily so strong that it overcomes all opposition. If a person wishes sufficiently strongly to believe something unreasonable, he will be able to stifle his critical faculty, though not with such ease as someone in whom it is less developed. Similarly, the curiosity or love of truth which the educated person acquires will make him eager to arrive at the most reasonable solution he can to moral questions, even those which do not at present concern him; but it may not be so strong that it overcomes a strong vested interest in *not* thinking some moral problem out.

We suggest, then, that both our theses are true. In other words, education is conducive to morality in two ways: through moral education as such – which is an important and distinct branch of education, even though it is not usually taught as a separate 'subject' – a pupil comes to understand what morality is, to appreciate moral arguments and to make moral judgments for himself; and through the rest of his education he acquires the knowledge and the means of gaining further knowledge, without which his moral judgments would sometimes be ill-informed, together with the critical disposition and love of truth which will lead him, in this field as in any other, to reject spurious argument and seek well-founded conclusions.

But this account shows only that education is a *necessary* condition of the highest moral possibilities, not that it is a *sufficient* condition. For our account so far explains how education helps us to know what to do; but to know what to do is not the same as doing it. To translate moral knowledge into action requires various qualities of character, depending on the circumstances; courage, self-control, perseverance, concern for others, love of justice, strength of will and so on. Nothing we have said gives us any reason to suppose that education, as we have described it, promotes these qualities at all.

This depressing conclusion will be strenuously rejected by those who espouse the Socratic view that 'virtue is knowledge' – that if we really know what we ought to do we must in fact do it. But the Socratic view is in fact rather difficult to defend, unless we give a very loaded account of 'knowing what to do' such that nothing is allowed to *count* as such knowledge unless it leads to action. If we do not resort to such a contrivance, however, it seems to be a commonplace of life that people can have the clearest possible idea of what they ought to do and yet fail to do it. The most we can say is that holding a moral position involves *some* attraction towards what is prescribed in it, as we said earlier.

It may be objected that our account of education is not as intellectualistic as the foregoing argument would suggest – that we have throughout insisted that part of education is the cultivation of certain inclinations, and that in the moral sphere these inclinations may be of the kind which lead to the right action. There is a good deal in this contention, but before we can examine its validity we must distinguish between two kinds of inclination in the sphere of morality. One may be called 'intellectual inclination within the moral sphere': this is the determination to arrive at a true moral view of things, to think things out carefully, reject spurious arguments and so on. The other is moral inclination proper: the inclination (if this is the word) to do what is right as such, together with aspects of this such as a love of justice and of veracity and the more 'natural' but still moralized passions such as concern for others' welfare. Both types of inclination may be called 'rational passions', to borrow a term from P. H. Hirst and R. S. Peters,[1] but they seem to be different in kind. It is the *first* kind of rational passion which seems part of the educated person by definition, and the first kind only that we previously mentioned in connexion with moral education.

Now this division is to some extent an artificial one, because

[1] Hirst and Peters, op. cit., pp. 39, 51.

underlying the intellectual inclinations in the moral sphere we would normally expect to find the moral inclinations proper. In other words, the reason why a person is keen to work out exactly what it would be just to do in a given situation is usually because he is keen on justice as such, and the reason why a teacher wishes to inculcate these intellectual inclinations is usually that he is a lover of morality, not merely of moral philosophy. But the distinction is worth making, because it enables us to allow for the existence of the educated but morally cynical, and the educated but morally feeble, who certainly exist and often are capable of penetrating and subtle moral judgments. Such people can be said to possess the first kind of rational passion in connexion with morality but not the second, and there seems nothing illogical about this description. It follows that we can assert that an educated person is likely to think more clearly on moral issues (which seems plausible) without being committed to saying that he is bound to behave better (which seems false).

We have just said that the passions which form part of moral educatedness are intellectual rather than moral. But it does not follow that a teacher does not, or that he should not, endeavour to inculcate the moral passions also. What does follow is that such an endeavour is more naturally called something other than 'education' – perhaps 'inspiration' is the natural word. This distinction may not however be merely verbal. A particular teacher may be able to transfer a love of truth and cogency from other spheres to the moral sphere without being able to make his pupils care about morality, and *vice versa*. *How* love of the moral good is transmitted is an empirical question of great complexity. It may be that it can be 'caught' off a loved teacher, but whether the teacher *qua* teacher is in any special position here (as opposed to, say, the parents) is rather doubtful. Claims are also made for the inspirational qualities of particular school subjects – for example, the arts and literature. But is it clear that beauty in art is really an aid to beauty of conduct (despite Plato)[1] or that literature necessarily makes us care more about real human beings?

It might well be suggested at this point that one potent source of moral inspiration has been omitted here: the school itself, and the

[1] Plato, *Republic*, 400E–402C.

smaller units, house, form and so on, within it. It is in relation to these microcosms of society (the suggestion continues) that a child first acquires the desire to serve a *community* bound to him by no natural ties; and this is the basis of morality. Now this may well be true in many cases. But this feature of school life is nothing to do with its *educational* purposes; it follows from the very fact that it is a community. From this particular point of view, inspiration may equally be forthcoming from a non-educational community, such as a youth club or sports club, and indeed such non-educational bodies may more readily win the relevant kind of allegiance from some children.

The same kind of point may be made in relation to the qualities, mentioned earlier, which are as necessary as inspiration to the moral life but which we have not discussed in detail: those qualities which seem particularly connected with the *will*, such as courage, self-control, patience, tenacity, etc. It might be argued that, just as the school community is the source of inspiration to public-spiritedness, so it provides the opportunity for the practice of these other virtues. But although schools have often prided themselves on inculcating such things – on the 'character training' they provided – there seems no reason why the *educational* community should be the prime source of them. Of course 'difficult' school subjects, such as mathematics and Latin, were often thought to be 'good for the character' in this way. But apart from the question whether it is *legitimate* to view such subjects as training grounds for the will, we can ask whether this feature of difficulty has any necessary connexion with aspects of education. We can perhaps agree that it is good for the character to do difficult things; but there are difficult things to do which are not part of education at all, and in any case not everyone finds Latin and mathematics difficult.

Our position on education and moral goodness may be summed up as follows. We hold that there is such a thing as moral education, which is conducive to morally good conduct and indeed necessary for the highest reaches of such conduct, though it has its own dangers; its function is to help the moral agent to form well-founded moral judgments. We think that other aspects of education may help also, in providing the factual knowledge often needed if a person is to come to a sound moral conclusion, and in cultivating the general critical disposition and love of truth which will sharpen his moral thinking. But we maintain that all of these intellectual capacities and inclinations, though necessary, are not sufficient for the highest moral conduct. For this other qualities are needed also, which seem to have no necessary connexion with education at all, though there may be contingent connexions: a teacher may be a source of inspiration, but *qua* person rather than *qua* academic; a school may inculcate public spirit, but *qua* community, not *qua* educational establishment; study of a subject may develop the character, but *qua* demanding pursuit, not *qua* pursuit of knowledge.

Before we leave the topic of education as leading to moral goodness let us consider how far education can be justified because it is necessary for other phenomena generally taken to be morally good, such as personal relationships and religion. It might of course be argued that these two cases are in fact rather different from each other, on the grounds that an understanding of religion sufficient to raise it above the level of a superstitition needs a measure of religious education, whereas personal relationships need no such intellectual training. But in fact it is not clear that the difference between religion and personal relationships in this respect is more than one of degree. Both need a certain minimum level of intellectual cultivation (religion more than friendship) but neither needs what we would want to call education. Thus we can speak of the uneducated peasant's 'simple faith' as religion, provided he has some understanding – which need not be at all philosophical – of what he believes. Similarly we can speak of the friendships of children or of primitive people, provided only they have reached a stage where they have sufficient consciousness of themselves and others as individuals for the notion of friendship to apply. (We discuss friendship further in Chapter Six.)

It might be said here that even if education is not necessary for religion or personal relationships, it is still conducive to them, in the sense we employed earlier in connexion with morality: that is, it is necessary for the highest possibilities. In support of this claim it might be maintained that there must be 'more to' the religion of a St Augustine or a St Thomas, because of the quality of their intellect, than to that of a peasant; and similarly more to the friendship of those of cultivated mind who can share together the most rewarding pursuits. This contention perhaps has some truth in it, but, as in the moral case, a degree of education can be a hazard as well as an asset both in religion and in personal relationships, making people critical and analytical where they should be spontaneous. As an example of this danger, consider the account given by P. H. Hirst and R. S. Peters of development in social matters: they say that the 'socially developed person' is able to 'distance himself a bit from social facts and from his fellows and theorize about them', and give as an example the regarding of the foibles of one's friends 'in terms of some derivative of Freudian theory'.[1] Hirst and Peters see this as a good thing, but surely to regard one's friends in this way is if anything destructive of personal relationships, since it involves seeing them as types rather than individuals, or even as things rather than persons. We shall discuss these various kinds of attitude more fully in Chapter Six.

We conclude this section rather more optimistically than we did the previous one. While education is not sufficient, either for morality or personal relationships or religion, nor even necessary for their existence in some form, it is *conducive* to all three, in the sense of being necessary for their finest flowering. Provided the hazards to all three afforded by education can be avoided, this conduciveness seems to provide a fair measure of extrinsic justification. How to avoid the hazards while securing the benefits is a problem for the educational psychologist as much as for the philosopher; we have no space to deal with this problem here.

4 Education and the good of society

To some extent, of course, we have just been discussing this topic under the heading 'education and moral goodness'. For even if we allow that moral goodness has value in itself and is not just a means to an end, it is clear that it is also of great instrumental value in promoting harmony and co-operation in society. Insofar as

[1] Hirst and Peters, op. cit., p. 51.

education promotes morality, therefore, it promotes the good of society, in one sense of that expression.

But of course 'the good of society' can mean a great many different things in different contexts. In the context of education it sometimes means 'material prosperity' or at any rate 'freedom from want and misery'. To say education promotes the good of society in this sense is to say that the more educated the citizens are, the higher the standard of living. And it is often thought to be obviously true that education does promote the good of society in this way. An educated general public, it is said, can look after themselves better and manage an increasingly technological society; and we need as well as these the more highly educated engineers, scientists, doctors and so forth to maintain our system.

But it might be maintained here that material prosperity demands in the citizens not education but *training*: in the majority a foundation of know-how, enabling them to find their way around the complex society, and a few more highly-trained specialists to work in technical fields. Thus R. S. Peters imagines someone grasping the 'conceptual point' that what is passed on in education is regarded as having intrinsic value, and thereupon saying 'Well, I am against education then. We have no time for such luxuries. We must equip people for suitable jobs and train enough scientists and technicians to maintain an expanding economy.'[1] What is envisaged here is presumably a narrow concentrated procedure, where the end-product of usefulness is stressed and neither breadth of development nor the questioning critical spirit is demanded.

It seems likely, however, that this narrow 'vocational' programme, besides being non-educational, will not even serve its required purpose. For while the *status quo* can presumably be maintained by trained technicians, progress seems often to require precisely those qualities which we think of as belonging to the educated rather than the merely trained person: an ability to ask why a thing is done one way rather than another, to apply ideas in unexpected fields and so on. Again, discoveries of immense practical benefit often are made through sheer curiosity in the first place – the desire simply to find out about something for its own sake. If all a person's

[1] Peters, op. cit., p. 29.

efforts are directed by schooling towards trying to be useful, this impulse to discovery for its own sake may be inhibited rather than strengthened.

It might be objected that all we have argued for is that material prosperity may need scientists, engineers and other 'useful' people who are taught (insofar as it *can* be taught) to be creative rather than merely follow rules. We have not shown why achieving a high standard of living needs from anyone a knowledge of art or poetry or history. The answer is surely that in practice we do not conceive of the good of society in merely material terms at all; we think of a 'high quality of life' and not merely 'a high standard of living', and in order to achieve this quality the members of the society must be educated to the limits of their capacity.

We make this last assertion for three reasons. Firstly, an awareness of issues other than the purely material ones is needed, both in the technologists and in those who employ them – the community. Otherwise they produce things which are materially convenient but ugly or inhuman, and which in the end the community does not want; this is the case with much modern building. Now this reason construes 'the good of society' as 'what people want', and points out that in the end people want more than prosperity. But we might look on the good of society in a different light, as made up in some way of the good of individuals in the sense discussed in Section 1. This consideration underlies our second reason. If people are educated they contribute to each other's good, in this sense; for intellectual and aesthetic activities are often enhanced by being shared. This reason still depicts the good of society in individualistic terms, as an aggregate of the good of individuals – the point being that the education of an individual can be seen as part of not only his good, but also that of others. We might, however, look on society in more organic terms, and say thirdly that the good of society is a *whole* composed, like the beauty of a mosaic picture, from the variety and richness of its parts – the members – and that education is the process whereby both variety and richness are procured.

The conclusion of this section is the most encouraging so far for suggesting a justification of education in terms of one of its extrinsic ends. For education does seem to promote the creative impulses and the self-criticism which are bound up with the good of a society broadly and humanely conceived. We therefore venture the conclusion that education in our narrow sense may be said to be necessary for the good of society; the good society will always be the educated society. We cannot, however, say that education is also sufficient. For part of the good of society is its moral tone, and morality is also necessary for other social goods which depend on co-operation; and, as we have seen, people can be educated without being morally good. But insofar as education is a necessary condition of some social goods – perhaps those which are collectively known as 'civilization' – it can be justified not only as something good in itself (as we argued in Chapter Three) but also as something good for what it brings.

5 Ancillary and complementary aims

There is something odd in the very idea of attempting to justify education in terms of its ancillary or complementary aims. It will be remembered that a teacher's ancillary aim is to remove impediments to the pursuit of his intrinsic aim, education. How could the pursuit of this intrinsic aim be justified by the pursuit of other aims which are themselves justifiable only because they further the intrinsic aim? Would it not be as silly as attempting to justify the aim of going on holiday in terms of the ancillary aim of taking luggage? In a similar way, it might be said that it would be logically absurd to attempt to justify the pursuit of the intrinsic aim of the teacher in terms of complementary aims, since they are, by definition, neither a part of educatedness nor, like extrinsic aims, achieved through educatedness. This would be like attempting to justify burning down your house on the grounds that you are aiming at roasting a pig, like the Chinamen in Charles Lamb's essay.[1]

These objections to the attempt to justify education in terms of its ancillary or complementary aims are in the end valid ones. But the situation is slightly more complex than our analysis of it has

[1] Charles Lamb, 'A Dissertation Upon Roast Pig', in *Essays of Elia*.

suggested. Let us take a different sort of example. Let us suppose that for reasons of national security a government introduces compulsory national service for its young men. The intrinsic aim here is national security, but in making the young men into soldiers the government may find that it is also furthering the extrinsic aim of making better citizens of the youth. Equally, to further its intrinsic aim, the government may find that it is useful to have ancillary aims, such as providing medical treatment for unfit young men, teaching some to read and write and so on. Again, the government may have complementary aims, such as making good sportsmen of some soldiers. Now once the military crisis is over the maintenance of the intrinsic aim is no longer justifiable, but a government might feel that there was justification for continuing the system in terms of the erstwhile ancillary and complementary benefits. Note, however, that it cannot (logically) be called a system of *defence*, since that as such is now no part of its aims.

In a similar way, a government might feel that there was justification for maintaining a school and university system, not because it was a system of education, but because of the ancillary and complementary benefits. A school system provides a unique opportunity for improving the youth of the country in many ways which have nothing to do with education.

We have no quarrel with this sort of justification provided it is realized that what is being justified cannot (logically) be *education*; for what these arguments justify is a *school system*, in which education may have a place, but is not necessarily the dominant concern.

6 Conclusion

In this chapter we have tried to discover to what extent education can be justified by what can be achieved through it – its extrinsic ends. We were doubtful whether any general justification can be offered for it in terms of what it produces for the individual in the form of enjoyment, pleasure, happiness or the like because for such goods it is neither necessary nor sufficient. The attainment of moral goodness fared better as an extrinsic justification, for some measure of education is a necessary condition, not of all, but of the highest levels, of moral goodness. But no amount of education is a sufficient condition of moral goodness, and hence this form of justification has its limitations. The good of society, however, provides the strongest extrinsic justification for education, because education is necessary for the richness and variety in which the good of society partly consists. Finally, while we do not believe that the ancillary and complementary aims of education can logically be justificatory, they may provide additional social reasons for maintaining a system of education.

Chapter Five

The role of the teacher

We have already claimed in Chapter One that 'teacher' is a role-job. Now the concept of social role is frequently used by social scientists and social philosophers in ways which are neither clear nor consistent, so it is necessary, before discussing the role of the teacher, to distinguish different senses of the concept and to specify the sense in which we are using the idea of 'role' in this chapter. There are four senses of the concept in common use, and we shall begin by giving a brief outline of these senses.[1]

1 'Teacher' as a role-job

In the first sense, 'role' is used very widely as a class concept. Used in this way, 'role' is simply a means of labelling a group of individuals in virtue of certain properties they have in common; we can, in this sense, speak of the role of 'teacher', 'football fan', 'invalid', 'cyclist', 'chess-player', etc. This wide sense is not very helpful, for to say that a person has the role of 'teacher' (in this sense of 'role') adds nothing by way of description or explanation; it is simply to say that a person *is* a teacher.

The second sense of the concept is more specific and brings out the dramatic associations of 'role'. Using the analogy of the 'types'

[1] For a discussion of the concept of social role see Eileen M. Loudfoot, 'The Concept of Social Role', *Philosophy of the Social Sciences*, 1972.

of the morality plays of the later middle ages, some social scientists speak of a person as 'playing the role of' or 'acting the part of' X or Y. To play the role of teacher or student is to see oneself as a teacher or a student and to expect other people to behave accordingly. This notion of 'playing a role' or 'acting a part' can be exemplified in different ways, and we shall consider how this may be done in Chapter Six; but it is not this sense of 'role' which is our concern in this present chapter.

Social scientists use the concept in a third sense, the sense of social function. In this case the analogy is with the biological sciences, and a person's role in society is viewed as the function he performs, the contribution he makes to the maintenance of the social system in an enduring state. The social scientist experiences certain difficulties in specifying the enduring state of society, the social system and its elements, and the nature of the causation involved. But let us assume that these difficulties are not insuperable and that we can speak of the role of 'teacher' or of the educational system and mean their causal function in society. 'Role' in this sense of 'causal function' could then be used in extrinsic justifications of education of the kind we considered in Chapter Four. For example, it might be argued that an educational system can be justified insofar as it has the role or function of transmitting the basic values which are necessary for the continuance of a given civilization. Used in this sense, 'role' is a *de facto* concept: it is concerned with the actual effects of a person or an institution in society, and makes no reference to the conscious purposes for which an institution was set up or to the way in which a person himself regards what he is doing. If we wish to bring in the internal or agent aspect we have to turn to the fourth sense of role.

'Role' in this fourth sense is a *de jure* concept, and is defined in terms of a set of rights and duties. It is these rights and duties which describe and explain the operation of institutions and which tell us why a certain person – say, a policeman, an income tax inspector or a teacher – in a certain position in society may legitimately do certain things. It is not, of course, denied that the execution of a duty can have a certain effect in society, but the point is that the person or institution with a role in the 'social function' sense need not be aware of this role, whereas the person who has a role in the 'rights and duties' sense of the term must be aware that he has it. We might say that in the 'social function' sense of 'role' a person can be said in fact to *have* a role, whereas in the 'rights and duties' sense of 'role' he can be said to be *in* a role, or to accept or reject a role. It is this latter sense of 'role', the 'rights and duties' sense, which is our concern in this chapter, and we shall now investigate the rights and duties of the teacher.

2 *The rights and duties of the role of 'teacher'*

We have agreed that part of what is involved in being a teacher is the possession of skill, and that part of what is involved is the pursuit of an aim. But not only does the teacher *qua* teacher possess skill and pursue a certain aim, the individual teacher also has a *right* to perform certain kinds of activities, and a *duty* to do certain things rather than others. But before we discuss to whom the teacher has these duties and against whom he has these rights it is important to distinguish the particular *kind* of rights and duties which go to make up the role of 'teacher'. The important distinction for our purposes is between what we may call *determining* and *accessory* rights and duties.[1] Determining rights and duties are those which determine an official position or sphere of action of a person in society; they are the rights and duties which define the nature of the position itself or which constitute the role. Clearly it is determining rights and duties which we have been intending when we have spoken of a role as a set of rights and duties. Accessory rights and duties are those which arise for a person because he already occupies a particular position in society. Accessory rights and duties do not determine the role but arise, or may arise, for a person because he has the role in question. For example, it is not part of the role of a clergyman to open the church fête, but it might be said to be an accessory duty. In a similar way it need not be one of the determining or constitutive duties of a teacher that he should take part in various extracurricular activities with his pupils, but it might be

[1] Loudfoot, op. cit., pp. 135–6.

said that this is an accessory duty. We shall discuss some of the accessory duties of the teacher in the next chapter. What we must now consider is the content of the role of the teacher, to whom he owes determining duties and against whom he has determining rights.

The use of the phrase 'content of the role of the teacher' suggests that what the teacher may and may not do, must and must not do, can be specified in detail. This, of course, is not the case, for the rights and duties which make up the role of a teacher will to some extent depend on a contract of employment which will not be uniformly applicable. But not all determining rights and duties are of this kind; it is possible to distinguish two general kinds of determining rights and duties in terms of their *source*. We can distinguish between determining rights and duties which have their origins in a contract of employment, i.e. *contractual* determining rights and duties, and determining rights and duties which derive from the nature or aims of teaching, i.e. *implicational* determining rights and duties. The former may vary from school to school, from education authority to education authority; the latter exist uniformly for every teacher, since they are rights and duties which any person who professes to teach will have, simply in virtue of the aims of teaching. Let us begin by considering contractual determining rights and duties.

Some of these rights and duties might be stated in detail, insofar as they might concern conditions of employment such as salary, vacations, working hours, etc., but others will be less precisely stated and lay down in general terms that a teacher will have a duty to undertake such work as his head of department or headmaster shall think fit. What the head of department or headmaster thinks fit may itself be specified in detail or may be left fairly general and open to interpretation by individual teachers. Still other duties may be even less precisely specified and may consist in indications of the ends to which the teacher should direct his activities and towards which the process of education is seen as being directed. These contractual rights and duties will for the most part be held against and owed to the employer. Now in most cases 'the employer' will be the local education authority or board of governors (although in certain cases the employing body could be the headmaster himself), but apart from being legally employed by either of these, the teacher may have little or no contact with such bodies. Rather, his contact will be with the headmaster or headmistress of the school in which he teaches. Does the teacher have determining duties to and rights against the headmaster or headmistress, where he or she is not also the employer?

We can answer this question in the affirmative if we say that the headmaster or headmistress is authorized to act by the employing body, so that the teacher has duties indirectly to the headmaster or headmistress as the agent or representative of the employing body. If, however, the headmaster exceeds his authority or acts outside his legal competence, then the teacher would have no determining duties to him in that given case, although for a variety of possible reasons he may accede to the headmaster's demands. It must be emphasized that there is a distinction between the headmaster's acting outside his legal competence and the headmaster's acting within his legal competence but implementing policies of which the teacher disapproves or with which he disagrees. This latter situation we shall discuss in Section 4 of this chapter. Let us now turn to implicational determining rights and duties.

We have described these as rights and duties which any person who professes to teach will have by virtue of the aims of teaching. Implicational duties, we shall claim, are owed by the teacher to the pupils, to society and to the subject-matter, while implicational rights are held by the teacher against the pupils, their parents and society at large. But what is the nature of these rights and duties?

Beginning with the notion of duties to the pupils, we can say that the teacher, by virtue of being a teacher, has a duty to the pupils to educate them. In arguing for this we can begin from the utilitarian premise that everyone has a duty to benefit society, to promote the welfare of others, etc. This duty is most efficiently performed, however, not by unorganized individual effort but by a division of labour whereby each individual makes some part of the general welfare his special concern. The machinery whereby this is organized is the institution in society of various roles or positions, the incumbents of which fulfil certain specifiable needs of the community or some part of the community. Insofar as a person accepts one of these roles, he has a duty to those whose needs the role is intended to fulfil. 'Teacher' is one such role, and is intended to fulfil the educational needs of a certain section of the community. The person who accepts the role of teacher has, therefore, a duty to fulfil the educational needs of those who have them.

The fact that the teacher has a duty of this kind to his pupils will put certain restrictions on the kind of methods he may use and, more generally, on the kinds of things he may do in the classroom. That is, if a teacher allows pupils to read novels instead of attempting to teach them history, he is failing in his duty towards the pupils – though this is not necessarily to say that the reading of certain novels may not be an aid towards historical education. Again, if a teacher insists on rote-learning to the extent that pupils are turned away from his subject, then he has failed in his duty towards the pupils, since he has failed to go even part of the way to fulfilling his duty to educate them.

Two objections might be raised to this line of argument. The first is that we have not so far spoken of education as a *need*. But there is no great difficulty in explaining the use of such a word. Of course education is not a physical need like food, something which people have to have in order to live. But the arguments of Chapters Three and Four show the kind of thing which might be meant here: education can be seen as a part of a man's self-realization, and as a part of his good or welfare; it is also conducive (in the sense we discussed in Chapter Four) to his moral life, his religion and his personal relationships. If these things are seen as important goods the lack of which makes a man unfortunate, we can reasonably speak of his need for education.

The second objection is that our line of argument makes the teacher's duty to the pupils a kind of derivative duty dependent on his duty to society, whereas this is not how we would naturally see such a duty. To examine the force of this argument, consider an analogy. Our society (as opposed, say, to ancient Sparta, Plato's ideal republic, or the more extreme Israeli kibbutzim) looks after the welfare of its children by means of the institution of the nuclear family, with the role of parent built into it. If our arrangements were different, parents would not have the duties they at present do. But does this fact make a parent's duties to his children derivative from a prior duty to society? Only in the sense that a parent can see his general duty to others as fulfilled primarily in fulfilling his duty to his children; they are the part of society which he is called on to serve, though he need not look at the situation like this. Similarly, a teacher who says that he wants to 'do his bit for society' can be told that he is doing just this in serving his pupils. Notice, however, that in educating his pupils the teacher is also promoting the good of society in another sense which goes beyond the pupils' own good, just as a parent who brings his children up well confers a benefit through them on the community at large, as well as on them as part of the community. For we argued in Chapter Four that educated citizens are conducive to the good of society as a whole. If this is true, the teacher's duty to educate the pupils can be seen not only as a duty to them but also as a duty to the rest of society: the duty to leaven it with educated citizens, a good for society which the teacher can help to produce.

We have spoken so far of the teacher's duties to the pupils and to society. It can also be claimed that the teacher has rights against the pupils or, in other words, that the pupils have duties to the teacher. This claim can be argued for in a number of different ways. First of all we can say that the teacher is in a position of authority in an institution whose existence is justified in terms of its ends and effects. Insofar as the pupil is a member of this institution, he has a duty to obey the instructions of the teacher to the extent that these instructions come within the scope of the teacher's authority. Note however that the pupil's institutional position can mean different things in different contexts. The university student's duties can be seen partly as contractual or quasi-contractual. He joins the institution of his own choice and may be deemed to consent thereby to the authority of those in authoritative positions. The school pupil, however, is not at school from choice, and his duties to the teacher cannot be in any sense contractual; they can be justified only in terms of the ends and effects served by the institution in which the teacher holds authority, in other words, by reference to the same quasi-utilitarian considerations on which we grounded the implicational duties of the teacher. These considerations serve also as added justification for the university student's duties to his teachers.

The second argument for the view that pupils have duties to teachers rests on the previous assertion that teachers have a duty to educate. In general, insofar as a person has a duty to do something, he has a right not to be obstructed or hindered by others in the course of doing his duty. So in this case, if the teacher has a duty to promote education he has a right against the pupils to a measure of co-operation from them.

Neither of the foregoing arguments commits us to saying that the pupil must on all occasions defer to the teacher. At least in the context of older age groups pupils themselves may raise the question of whether on certain occasions the teacher is acting outside his sphere of authority, or whether he is in fact pursuing or even attempting to pursue his duty; the claim here is merely that insofar as the teacher is acting within his sphere of authority or is pursuing his duty, the pupils have duties to him.

There is a third way in which it is possible to argue that the pupils have duties to the teacher, although this way makes these duties derivative rather than direct. This third argument is based on the claim that people have the general duty to develop their capacities to the fullest extent. Such a duty might be seen either as a case of the duty to produce what is good in itself (educatedness being seen as such a good, as we argued in Chapter Three) or as a duty to oneself in respect of one's own true good or welfare, in the way considered in Chapter Four. Assuming the existence of such a duty, on either ground, the pupil has a derivative duty to do whatever is conducive to the fulfilment of the primary duty. Hence he has a duty to listen to the teacher because the teacher helps him to fulfil his duty to develop his capacities.

That the pupils have duties to the teacher may seem acceptable in the case of older pupils, but doubts may be raised about whether this can be the case with younger pupils. Is it plausible to suggest that five- or six-year-old children have duties to the teacher? Here the answer has to be that it depends on the child in question. Some young children are quite able to understand the idea of duties of this kind, while others are not. But in the case of young children we can say in more general terms that the teacher in virtue of his duties has rights against the *parents* of the children, and they have duties not to hinder the teacher in the fulfilment of his responsibilities. These rights against the parents may include the right that the parents try to ensure that the child is reasonably well-behaved, that his homework is supervised, that he is not in any way discouraged from pursuing tasks which are set him, that his interest in subjects of educational value is fostered. These rights against the parents also hold in the case of older pupils: that is, in addition to the duties of the pupils to the teacher there are duties of the parents not to hinder teacher and pupil in the pursuit of their duties. Similarly we can argue that society at large has a duty not to hinder teacher and pupil – though it would take too long to work out all the implications of this notion. Let us now turn to the idea that the teacher has duties to his subject-matter.

It may seem strange to speak of the teacher as having a duty to his subject-matter: can one speak of 'a duty to history' or 'a duty to mathematics'? Indeed, there are certain philosophical arguments which can be raised against the idea that it is possible to have duties to non-personal entities.[1] These difficulties may be avoided if instead of saying that the teacher has duties to history, etc. we say that the teacher has duties *concerning* history, etc. or, putting it more generally, the teacher has duties concerning his subject-matter. The idea of duties concerning the subject-matter might be summed up if we said that the teacher ought to show respect for his subject in his treatment of it. For example, he ought not to be derogatory, frivolous or cynical or in other ways degrade the subject (say by using learning techniques such as jingles) in his teaching of it. Rather he ought to teach it with enthusiasm as something worthwhile and worthy of study; and if he himself clearly shows respect for the subject in his treatment of it he will encourage the appropriate response in his pupils.

In this section we have discussed the contractual and implicational determining rights and duties which make up the role of the teacher. We now wish to raise the question of the *means* which the

[1] See R. S. Downie and Elizabeth Telfer, *Respect For Persons*, pp. 80–81 (London, Allen and Unwin, 1966).

teacher may employ in carrying out the duties of his role. We have argued that the pupils have various duties to the teacher, but these are very often ignored or not even recognized as such. When this happens, is the teacher entitled to compel pupils to do certain things against their wishes? Is such compulsion educationally desirable? Other questions may be raised about the *extent* of the teacher's rights against the pupils: are these limited by the pupils' right at least to be consulted about curricula or choice of textbooks, or about the enforcement of discipline? In short, the problems which now arise can be said to be those connected with compulsion and paternalism in the school context and these we shall now discuss.

3 Paternalism

The compulsion which takes place in schools and colleges is often described or stigmatized, rightly or wrongly, as paternalistic, and we cannot discuss compulsion without discussing paternalism. The topic of the justification of paternalism in the sphere of education (or the lack of justification) is one which is very much to the fore at present. For example, the National Council for Civil Liberties has mounted a campaign for children's rights in the educational field,[1] and the National Union of Teachers has replied with criticisms of the 'unrealistic policies' put forward by the NCCL.[2] Generalizing, we might say that the NCCL is against at least some kinds of paternalistic action towards pupils, whereas teachers have insisted that at least some measure of paternalistic action is necessary. In this section, then, we wish to examine these claims. Before this can be done, however, we must have a clear idea of what is meant by 'paternalism'.

The terms 'paternalism' and 'paternalistic' tend to be used in a pejorative sense. That is to say, contained in the meaning of these terms as used in everyday speech is a value judgment to the effect

[1] National Council for Civil Liberties, *Children Have Rights*, no. 1: 'Children in Schools'.
[2] *The Observer*, 30 April, 1972.

that paternalistic interference is always wrong or is necessarily a bad thing. But we can give a descriptive definition of paternalism, which leaves open the question of justification. Such a definition is 'the protection of individuals from self-inflicted harm, or their direction towards their own good or interests'.[1] The notions of harm and interests are of course extremely wide and vague ones which we cannot discuss in general here. For our present purposes, however, we can concentrate on the kind of good discussed in Chapter Four: viz. that the achievement of educatedness might be seen as forming part of a man's own good or welfare, not because he wants it or is made happier by it, but because of what it is in itself and because of the other important things it brings him. In the context of education, then, paternalism is centrally the directing of pupils towards this aspect of their good, though since schools concern themselves with things other than education they may well 'direct' pupils towards other goods as well. 'Directing' is of course a vague word, like the other word 'interference' often used in this context. But this vagueness may be an advantage: it allows us to include all the forms of pressure which teachers put on pupils to do things which they otherwise would not do.

The important feature of paternalism, in terms of which paternalistic interference is distinguished from other kinds of interference with people's actions, is that any interference which can correctly be described as 'paternalistic' logically must be intended to protect the person interfered with or to conduce to his welfare. Thus it is not paternalistic to interfere with a person's actions in order to protect his family or the community. Many restrictive rules are wrongly described as 'paternalistic' by those who wish to criticize them or reject them, and this kind of mistake occurs frequently in the school context. For example, rules often regarded as paternalistic are those such as 'Curriculum, discipline, etc. shall be decided by the teachers and head teachers' and 'The editor, who shall be a member of the teaching staff, shall make the final decision on con-

---

[1] For discussions of paternalism, see Basil Mitchell, *Law, Morality and Religion in a Secular Society*, ch. V (London, Oxford University Press, Oxford Paperbacks, 1967); Joel Feinberg, *Social Philosophy* (New Jersey, Prentice-Hall, 1973).

tributions to the school magazine'. Such rules are often defended by saying that 'teacher knows best'. But such a defence is not *per se* paternalistic; it is so only if the added claim is made that the teacher's knowledge shall override any view or opinion of the pupil *in the pupil's own interests*. It is *not* paternalistic for the English teacher to have the final say on the school magazine on the grounds that he knows more about editing, literary journalism, the idiosyncrasies of printers, etc. Nor is it paternalistic to censor contributions on the grounds that they are critical of certain established institutions or customs within the school. Whether or not the latter should be done raises the problem of freedom of expression within the school context, but we shall not discuss this here. The point is simply that not all curtailment of freedom is paternalistic.

The same point can be stressed by contrasting 'paternalism' with another concept with which it tends to be confused. This concept is that of 'authoritarianism'. Paternalistic interference and authoritarian interference clearly have in common the fact that both are aimed at restricting freedom of action. The difference between the two concepts lies in the grounds given for the interference. We have said that for interference to be paternalistic the interference (logically) must be aimed at protecting a person and his interests. By contrast, authoritarian interference need not, and characteristically does not, have any such aim. The ground for authoritarian interference is that the person doing the interfering claims the right to do so and claims that no further ground need be given. Colloquially the point may be made by saying that the reason given for paternalistic interference is 'It's for your own good', whereas the reason given for authoritarian interference is 'because *I* say so'.

It will by now be clear that the purposes of those who interfere with children's freedom in the context of education are by and large paternalistic in the sense we have discussed. There are particular cases as we have just mentioned where other considerations are relevant, but by and large the dominant consideration is the good of the child. At a general level, the idea is that he should be compelled to be educated for his own good. Within that general aim, which parents, teachers and government pursue, it is thought that particular things (subjects, books, etc.) are vital to education and hence to the good of the child, and so these also are imposed for paternalistic reasons. It is true that the good of society plays some part in the justification of education, as we saw in the previous chapter. But where, as is usually the case, the good of society is seen as subordinate to the good of the individual in justifying the imposition of education on him, we have a case of paternalistic interference. We said earlier that 'paternalism' tends to carry a pejorative significance; we must now consider why this is so and whether the paternalistic interference of the teacher can nevertheless be justified.

The basis of the hostility to paternalism is the liberal doctrine to the effect that no one has a right to interfere with another except to prevent harm to, or perhaps to promote the good of, a third party:[1] in other words, A is not justified in interfering with B simply in order to do B good. This doctrine rests in turn on two ideas: that very often B is the best judge of his own good, and that even where this is not so he has a basic right as a human being to make his own mistakes and decide things for himself. To interfere paternalistically, then, is both to imply that you know another's business better than he does himself and to deny him the human right of liberty to make his own mistakes. Very often of course the interferer does not know what would be good for another, or even if he does he is not justified in infringing his liberty; in these cases paternalism is not justified. But it is not unjustified by definition, for there are cases where another party is better qualified to judge what constitutes a person's good than the person himself, and where the right to make one's own mistakes is overridden by other vital considerations or not fully present. Where both these conditions obtain a measure of paternalism is justified, and we hold that the educational situation is one such case. Let us briefly consider the claim that the conditions for justified paternalism obtain in the educational situation.

The first condition is that the interferer must know better than the object of interference what his good is. In the teacher's case we can defend this condition by pointing out that the teacher has certain

[1] J. S. Mill, *On Liberty*, ch. I, p. 135 et passim (London, Collins, The Fontana Library, 1962).

abilities by virtue of which he can be regarded as an authority or expert on certain subjects. Because he has this expert knowledge the teacher knows what is required as a condition of educatedness. Thus he can claim that he has a right to impose his demands for the good of the pupils, and that he can pursue their good by selecting material which must be learned and by attempting to make the pupils learn this material.

It might be objected to this defence of the first condition that in the field of education there can be no experts, and consequently that the teacher does not know what is for the good of the pupils. Now as far as certain subjects are concerned – science or history, say – the objection is implausible. Such subjects admit of a degree of precision which justifies the use of the idea of expertise, and insofar as a teacher is himself properly educated he will therefore, relatively to the pupils, be an expert. Moreover, even in fields where the idea of an expert is not a happy one – the appreciation of literature and the arts, say – the properly educated teacher will have an informed judgment which qualifies him to express views on these subjects to which the pupil ought to defer. To maintain this is quite compatible with maintaining at the same time that the teacher ought also to convey in his teaching that even the greatest experts can err, and that informed opinion is different from knowledge.

We have been speaking of expertise and informed judgment as far as the *subject* is concerned. A teacher, however, possesses expertise in the rather different matter of putting the subject across to his pupils – that is, in the *skills* of teaching. Such skills in pedagogy entitle a teacher to decide matters such as the order in which it is best for the pupils that a subject should be tackled. For example, experience might tell him that most pupils find a certain area of mathematics relatively easier and that it should therefore come before another area which pupils find relatively harder. Again, a teacher on the basis of his pedagogical skills may be entitled to decide that it is for the good of the pupils that the study of Shakespeare should be postponed till the pupils have reached a certain age, or that the learning of French is best begun in the primary school. (It is worth noting *en passant* that there may be a tension in certain subjects, especially mathematics, between the expertise of the teacher *qua* scholar and his expertise *qua* pedagogue. Thus, the *logical* order in which one theorem follows another may be different from the *pedagogical* order in which they are best presented to the pupils.) We therefore maintain that insofar as a teacher is a proper teacher he will have the knowledge of his subject and the skills in teaching it which entitle him to decide what is best for his pupils to learn in respect of the content and order of school subjects.

The objection to the view that a teacher is an expert might be pressed in a slightly different way. It might be argued that even if the teacher is an expert both in his subject and in his ability to present it to his pupils there remain the fundamental questions: the extent to which certain subjects should be taught in schools, and indeed whether education is a good at all. As far as these basic questions are concerned, it might be argued, the teacher is no expert, for there cannot be experts on such questions. The reply to this objection is that, while it is true that we cannot here speak of experts because there is not sufficient agreement, the teacher is judging these matters from a position of experience and maturity relative to the pupils. Indeed, the judgments which are relevant here are not merely those of given teachers, but those expressed in 'the accumulated wisdom of mankind' on the value of learning and on what is worth learning: some subjects, as we have already argued in Chapter Two, constitute the structure of mankind's grounded knowledge. This is not an argument for lack of adventure in the choice of what is taught or the methods of teaching it, but it is an argument for saying that some views on these matters are more likely to be worth listening to than others, and that the teacher's are more likely to be worth listening to than the pupil's.

The second condition for justified paternalism is that the normal right of non-interference is overridden or not fully present. To sustain this claim in the case of school pupils is a complex and controversial matter, resting on a view of children as not fully persons, or as potential persons, who do not as yet possess the full measure of human rights.[1] This does not mean that they have *no* rights, only that we normally make a distinction between the extent of the rights of a child to decide his own life and the rights of

[1] See Downie and Telfer, op. cit., pp. 34–5.

an adult. Of course the degree of this limitation of children's rights depends on the age of the child. But then this is commonly recognized in educational practice. A teacher will often say to an older child 'If you want to drop Latin, it's your funeral', or 'If you fool around in my lessons instead of listening, that's up to you' – thus implying that there are certain decisions which the child has a right to make, wisely or stupidly as the case may be, for himself. With this qualification we accept the second condition of justified paternalism in the context of education. Our argument then is that paternalism is justifiable on the part of the teacher, to the extent that he may select the material which is to be learned for the pupils' own good and attempt to make them learn it.

As an amplification of this conclusion it might be said that the pupil ought to be listened to and that the teacher ought to take the trouble to explain why certain subjects are taught or taught in a certain way; otherwise the pupil might refuse to learn, or to learn as well as he might do if he were co-operative. In other words, consultation and discussion can be encouraged within paternalism because they create an atmosphere friendly to learning; there are limits, as we saw in Chapter Two, to the extent to which someone can be *made* to learn.

To justify discussion and consultation in this way is of course to make it a means to learning and in no way to qualify the extent of justified paternalism in education. It can however be argued that the pupil has certain minimum *rights* to consultation – that he ought to be allowed to participate to some extent in the decisions, etc., which determine the educational policies of his school. If he has such minimum rights they will qualify the degree to which the paternalistic approach is justified. Let us now turn to this topic.

4 Participation

There seem to be two different kinds of issue with which the pupils of a school (or the students of a university) might be concerned: the content and method of the teaching syllabus and the formulation and enforcement of rules. There is a tendency to discuss these together in the context of the participation of pupils, but it is arguable that distinctions must be drawn between them with regard to the possibility and desirability of pupil participation. Let us look first of all at the content and methods of the teaching syllabus.

It would seem reasonable to say that in the early stages of their career pupils do not have the necessary knowledge to make any decisions about the content of their courses. But it also seems not unreasonable to say that by the time a pupil has reached the fifth or sixth form his competence has increased sufficiently for him to have a valid point of view. But here we must be cautious about the interpretation of 'having a valid point of view'. Does this mean simply that the pupils have a right to express a preference or offer an opinion, or does it mean that if sufficient numbers of pupils express a desire for change, change should ensue? It cannot automatically be the latter, for the reasons that the preference expressed may be seen by someone more knowledgeable to be a silly one, and that in any case the head teacher is ultimately responsible for the content and subject-matter of courses and must therefore take the final decisions with regard to them. Perhaps, however, before doing so he ought to take the views of his pupils and colleagues into consideration; in other words, between the two extremes there can be consultation.

The degree and extent of the consultation with pupils that is possible will obviously vary from subject to subject. But pupils can always be asked for their reactions to the textbooks they have used and their reasons for preferring one part of the syllabus to another. And even where the content of a course is not open to consultation a teacher should nevertheless try to *explain* to his pupils why it has been chosen. Consultation and explanation are again possible and desirable over the methods of teaching. Thus it may emerge from consultative procedures that pupils of different abilities and aptitudes prefer and learn more from different methods of teaching the same subject. Awareness of this kind of point can prevent frustration on the part of both pupil and teacher; again, if the pupil feels that he has been consulted with regard to these things, he may be more prepared to struggle with subjects or aspects of subjects which he finds difficult. Consultations of this kind can also aid the pupil in other ways. They can help him to acquire the skill of marshalling his arguments for a certain view in a cogent and coherent way, and they can also extend his understanding and tolerance by revealing to him the reasons for one decision rather than another and by making him aware of the difficulties involved in organization and decision-making.

But these reasons for allowing consultation are only part of the story. As we mentioned at the end of our previous section, they are themselves paternalistic in intent, suggesting that the pupils should be consulted only insofar as it is thought good for them by the teachers. It might also be said, however, that older pupils have a right to be consulted which sets a limit to the rights of the teachers; this right is what is left of their general right to non-interference when their youth and ignorance of the subject-matter have been set against it.

We come now to the formulation and enforcement of rules. There seems to be no reason why pupils or their representatives should not ask why a given rule exists or ask for its removal if they regard it as unnecessarily restrictive, though this is not to say that the rule should necessarily be removed. Knowing the reasons for the existence of a rule is often half-way to accepting the need for its existence. Nor does there seem to be any reason why pupils should not ask for a new rule to be made. As before, paternalistic reasons as well as appeal to pupils' rights can be used to defend the practice of consultation on the formulation of rules. But here the pupils' case for rights to non-interference is stronger than in the purely academic sphere; for the teacher's claim to be an expert who knows best what is the pupils' interest is more contentious outside the sphere of his academic competence. Many issues are raised here which we cannot possibly examine.

The *enforcement* of rules and punishment for their infringement raises some new problems. The claim of the NCCL is that the representatives of pupils should have some say in disciplinary matters.[1] In most schools, prefects or monitors do themselves have the right to inflict certain kinds of punishment for certain kinds of

[1] NCCL, op. cit.

offences. We would argue that the sphere of prefectorial or moni-torial discipline should be kept within strictly defined and narrow limits, for the following reasons. 'Punishment', it can be said, is a role-concept, in that for X to punish Y, X must be acting in a role or must have authority over Y. Similarly, for Y to accept that he has been *punished*, he must recognize that X is acting in a role. If prefects or monitors within a school are given wide-ranging author-ity, it becomes difficult for the ordinary pupil to distinguish the prefect acting in a role and punishing because he has a right – or a duty – to do so *qua* role-occupant from John Smith in the Sixth, who does not like him, deliberately 'getting at him'. This kind of situation can lead to difficulties of more than one kind. The ordi-nary pupil may come to resent prefectorial authority and the pre-fect may become alienated from his fellow pupils or may *as a person* become harsh and overbearing. All of these things not only lead to disharmony in the school but can also have a deleterious effect on the personality of the individuals concerned.

The claim of the NCCL and others that pupils should have some say in disciplinary matters is, however, rather different from the advocacy of the prefectorial system. The claim seems to be rather that in matters of discipline which have conventionally and tra-ditionally come under the aegis of the head teacher and other members of staff, pupils ought to play some part. But, irrespective of the meaning of 'some part', there are certain undesirable features about the presence of pupils on such occasions.

In the first place, whereas the NCCL sees the presence of pupils as offsetting some of the 'undesirable results of the head teacher's occasional autocratic decisions', as a matter of experience it seems to be the case that fellow pupils or students are at least as severe, if indeed not more so, as those whose decisions they are supposed to offset. And they may not be any less autocratic. Secondly, a pupil may not wish his wrongdoing to be made known to his fellow pupils, and may out of resentment become more wayward and truculent. Thirdly, there are all the difficulties which we have already mentioned in discussion of prefectorial authority – i.e. those difficulties associated with the distinction between personal action and role-enactment. Fourthly, if punishment is to be meted out by a disciplinary committee, this will necessarily involve a time-lag between the 'crime' and the punishment. This, it could be argued, is a bad thing, particularly in the case of nervous or highly-strung pupils. None of the above undesirable features provides conclusive argument against the participation of pupils in disciplinary matters, but these features suggest that such participation should not be advocated without due consideration. But it does not follow from this that the pupil must simply submit to any punishment meted out to him.

As we shall stress in the next section of this chapter, and in Chapter Six, the teacher is not simply a functionary. Rather he is a person acting in a role. This being the case, he will be subject to the same strains and stresses as all other persons. Thus he may punish in anger, when he is feeling out of sorts or when he is worried about his marriage or his work, or he may be irrational to the extent that he is obsessed by some small detail of work or behaviour which someone else would let pass unnoticed. Because the teacher is subject to such stresses and may have such obsessions, it is possible that he may on some occasion punish a pupil unjustifiably or too severely. To guard against this, it is arguable that there should be some means of redress for the pupils, some formal machinery through which an appeal can be made. And the possibility of such an appeal should not depend on contingencies such as the willingness of the headmaster to listen to a particular pupil on a particular day. The existence of such a means of appeal would have two advantages: firstly, it would make it clear to pupils that they are regarded as rational beings who might 'have a case', and secondly, it would put some restraint on the teacher who is too ready to punish or too severe – and such teachers certainly exist.

In summary of this section, we can say that the teacher, as expert or authority, knows what is for the good of the pupil and therefore has the right to select and impose material appropriate for the furtherance of this good. But, as we saw in Chapter Two, the teacher cannot guarantee to make the pupil an educated person. Although we have justified the selection of texts, etc., by the teacher in the pupil's interest, we have suggested that consultation with

pupils on certain issues can be both educationally valuable and part
of the pupils' rights.

5 Private views and public role (CONFLICT)

We have claimed that the individual teacher acts in a social role,
in the sense that he has certain official rights and duties which govern
his actions. It is equally the case that the individual teacher will have
certain personal beliefs and convictions, and these may come into
conflict with what he is required to do in his social role. If a teacher
finds his personal views in conflict with official requirements, how
should he resolve this situation? We cannot provide an answer for
every occasion, but what we will do here is to argue that certain
considerations are relevant to the making of decisions in this kind
of context. There are two kinds of situation in which conflict can
arise: vis-à-vis the headmaster, head of department or education
committee, and vis-à-vis the pupils. Let us begin by considering the
personal views of the teacher vis-à-vis the headmaster, etc.

Let us suppose that the teacher finds himself in the situation
where he morally disapproves of what he ought to do in his official
capacity. The problem may be, for example, that the teacher is in-
structed to inflict corporal punishment on a pupil or a number of
pupils, and he finds himself in moral disagreement with this course
of action. The problem is to analyse the principles which ought to
govern the conduct of the teacher when he finds himself in this
kind of position. One extreme view on this we might call the
'ignore-your-own-attitude' view. This is the view that any person
who has an official role – be he teacher, politician or social worker –
ought not to have a view of his own because it will have bad consequences if 'public servants' enact only those views with which they
personally agree. On this view any person with an official role
abdicates from responsibility for the actual policies carried out;
he becomes simply an implementer.

As against the 'ignore-your-own-attitude' view there is another
simple view of the situation which we may call the 'resign-if-you-
disagree' view. This is the view that if a person finds himself in

moral disagreement with the duties of his role or the policies he is expected to carry out in it he ought to resign the role. In this view a man is held responsible for the total action which proceeds from the role, as he would have been supposing he had also created both the structure of the role and the policy. Insofar as he did not bother to envisage the kind of actions which may be expected of him he is at fault. Thus, we might say to the teacher 'You ought to have gone into the implications of your job'. But a job can sometimes turn out to have unexpected features, and then the question of resignation arises. Thus we say 'You ought to resign rather than support such policies'. In other words, the argument admits that tensions may sometimes exist between the duties demanded by a person in his social role and his private moral beliefs, and claims that his private moral beliefs must in every case be given priority; he is fully responsible for the actions he performs in his role, as he is for his actions as a private person.

The 'resign-if-you-disagree' view makes an appeal to the liberal cast of mind. The decision to accept a role, on this view, in no way commits one morally to anything one would not otherwise decide to do, for there is always the escape of resignation. In support of this view its exponents might point to Eichmann as one who saw himself simply as an implementer of a policy he was bound to carry out in terms of the duties of his role. Their argument would be that 'I was only doing what I was told to do' is an excuse with a very limited acceptability; the individual ought always to think and decide for himself what he will do.

Now although the 'resign-if-you-disagree' view may sound plausible, there are several factors which may be urged against it, or in qualification of it. The first is that in the teaching situation frequent resignations make for bad educational consequences and hence are undesirable for the pupils and for the community as a whole. It is indeed a common complaint of parents that the education of pupils suffers if there is a high turn-over rate among those who are teaching them. It might be said against this qualification that this is an empirical question which can be settled only by looking at the evidence; but whether or not the evidence supports the qualification, the fact remains that people *believe* that continuity is necessary for good educational results, and since the co-operation of parents and others in the community is essential the beliefs of these people must be taken into account. If this qualification is accepted it can be suggested that over minor matters the 'ignore-your-own-attitude' view is a justifiable line for the teacher to take, since the consequences of resigning are worse than those of implementing the disputed policy.

Now it might here be admitted that frequent resignations are educationally bad and so not justified over minor issues. But the question can be raised as to who is to decide whether or not a point of dispute is 'minor' rather than 'major'. For example, in some areas of society corporal punishment might be accepted as the norm, but in others the infliction of such punishment might count as a major point of moral disagreement. It is almost impossible to legislate on this question, but some suggestions might be made. It might be said that in the school situation organization of classes and timetabling constitute 'minor' matters, and in disagreements on points such as these the teacher might be best advised simply to 'ignore his own attitude'. On the other hand, infliction of certain kinds of punishment and interference with the actual teaching of a class may constitute 'major' matters. Of course, what have been described as 'minor' matters may *become* 'major' if, for example, the teacher thinks that timetabling arrangements result in too little time's being given to a certain subject, with bad educational consequences. Thus it appears that although a rough line might be drawn between the organizational and the educational, the two in practice often come together. The suggestion which might be made is that the teacher should consider seriously whether his disagreement with his superiors is really important or whether he has, perhaps, laid too much stress on the importance of his own particular subject, or has simply become 'pig-headed'. At all events, the important point at issue might be said to be the 'good' of the pupils, and not the self-satisfaction of the teacher.

A second factor which may be urged against the unqualified 'resign-if-you-disagree' view is that resignation may have consequences which extend far beyond the particular matter over which the person resigned. For example, a teacher may resign over a matter of internal school politics, but this may have the effect of bringing the whole educational policy of the school into disrepute, which was in no way what the teacher intended. This possibility is by no means merely theoretical in view of the glare of publicity which can be turned on incidents in the educational world.

In the third place, it is important to consider the consequences that resignation will have on the role or policy which is being carried out. A person may dislike a particular syllabus or educational policy but still feel obliged to remain in his post because, by opting out, he will leave the role open for someone with less concern than he has. There are various ways in which a role can be enacted, and a person can bring to his actions a quality which may either mitigate or exacerbate its unfortunate effects.

A fourth point, and one which is related to the previous one, is that it is often easier to criticize and effect change from the inside rather than the outside, as it were. The teacher who resigns and then tries to campaign to have changes made is likely to find that the ranks have closed against him, and that he is considered to be an outsider who has no right to criticize. And if the teacher feels that certain changes ought to be made, it is his duty to go the best way about trying to implement these changes.

In view of these relevant considerations – the bad educational results which frequent resignations might produce, the possibility of unforeseen and unwanted repercussions, the possibility of moderating the bad effects of a role or policy by enlightened role-enactment – it seems clear that the 'resign-if-you-disagree' view cannot be accepted *simpliciter* but needs to be qualified by the 'ignore-your-own-attitude' view. As we have indicated, how far it must be qualified is a question for the individual teacher and depends on the particular situation in which he finds himself. A teacher might, however, apply three tests before deciding to resign. He should ask himself whether the issue is one of main principle rather than secondary matters; whether he himself will be directly involved in carrying out the decision; and whether the issue will present a continuing problem in which he will be expected to defend a view or a policy with which he is in fundamental disagreement. Only if the answer to all three questions is in the affirmative should the teacher resign. Of course any teacher might want to add to, or distinguish among, these tests; but clearly the moral situation for a teacher, or for anyone in a social role, has more complexity than emerged in the simple form of the 'resign-if-you-disagree' view.

Now it may be objected that to reject the simple form of the 'resign-if-you-disagree' view is also to reject the doctrine, funda-mental to the liberal-democratic attitude, that responsibility is an attribute of the adult individual; it is to admit that a person may sometimes perform actions which have elements in them for which he is not fully responsible. But this objection is based on a con-fusion over the doctrine of individual responsibility. The doctrine is that sane adult individuals (and no others) are to be held totally responsible for their actions: it is not that sane adult individuals are to be held responsible for the total content of their actions. To admit the need for modification in the 'resign-if-you-disagree' view is not to abandon the doctrine that responsibility is an attribute of the individual, but rather to draw attention to the problem for the agent which follows from its acceptance. The factors in terms of which we have modified the 'resign-if-you-disagree' view cer-tainly imply that for a teacher or for any other role-occupant the moral choice must sometimes be a choice between evils. For in-stance, the teacher may need to choose between resigning in pro-test and so leaving the role open for someone who cares less, and that of remaining in the role and so implementing a policy of which he does not approve. But a choice between evils is still a choice which can be made by a responsible person; no moral abdication is involved. After all, the situation of the private person not acting in a social role may occasionally be such that he must choose between evils, and we would not on that account alone deny him moral responsibility. Indeed, it may be said that the agent is never responsible for the total content of an action. The situation in which he finds himself is never one of which he is sole creator, since he is born into an environment not of his making; his moral actions, being reactions to his situation, are necessarily affected by it.

The second context in which there may be conflict between public or official demands and personal views is that of the role-relation-ship between teacher and pupil: it is easy for a teacher, or professor, to misuse his authority in certain subject-matters and so to obtain the agreement of impressionable pupils on what we may call his private views: various matters on which he is no more entitled to be listened to than the next man, or his pupils themselves.

The teacher may use the teaching situation as a vehicle for his private views in two ways. In the first place, he may put forward views on political or social matters which are unrelated to his teaching subject-matter; in extreme cases, he may view the pupils as suitable material for conversion to points of view in which he himself believes. Of course it is a good thing that a teacher should have views on matters other than on his own subject and should, when this is appropriate, disclose these to his pupils. It is a good thing because it is part of a person's education that he should hear a variety of opinions on many topics and because in indicating these opinions to his pupils the teacher will appear as a more rounded personality. We shall suggest in the next chapter that such revelation of his private views is part of the friendly behaviour which is an accessory duty of the teacher. But the putting forward of private views can nevertheless infringe the teacher's duty to his pupils, in three ways. Firstly, it may involve a failure in the teacher's duty to educate his pupils where, as in some extreme cases, promulgating private views on other subjects becomes a substitute for the teaching of history, mathematics or chemistry. Secondly, a pupil may be treated unfairly or victimized because he does not share the private views of the teacher. That is, the impartiality of the role sinks under the weight of personal bias. Nor need it even be the case that unfairness does actually result for the teaching relationship to be distorted. It is enough for pupils to believe that agreement with the teacher's personal views is a *sine qua non* of, say, a good report, for the carrying out of teaching duties to be in jeopardy. Thirdly, the teacher may, in extreme cases, be failing to treat the pupils as persons and simply viewing them as conversion fodder. In such cases the teacher is failing not only in his duty *qua* teacher, but *qua* moral agent, as we shall see in the next chapter.

We said that there were two ways in which a teacher might use the teaching situation as a vehicle for his private views. The second way is more insidious than the first in that it consists in presenting private views in the context of teaching a particular subject. Thus it is possible to teach fascism or anarchism while teaching history. Again, there are extreme and less extreme forms of this kind of practice. In the extreme form, a teacher may deliberately omit or distort facts in an attempt to prove his point. In the less extreme form he may more subtly 'colour' the facts, emphasize without argument some more than others and infiltrate his own evaluations in the guise of giving factual information. Of course, there is a place for evaluation – a criticism often made by students and pupils is that there is too much unsifted fact as opposed to evaluation – but such evaluation must be made on the basis of objective fact (where this exists) and must be argued for, and the pupil must be aware that other conclusions are possible. In other words, the views must be grounded and the pupil encouraged to be critical of them. If the teacher does use his subject-matter as a vehicle for his own private views, he may fall short of his duties to the pupil in the same three ways as before. He will be failing to educate the pupils as opposed to propagandizing them, he may treat unfairly or be believed to treat unfairly these pupils who do not adopt his own line on a subject, and he will be failing to respect his pupils as rational persons.

There are three antidotes to the *malaise* of over-obtrusive private views, which can be characterized in terms of different kinds of awareness. The first of these is the cultivation of the awareness that the pupil or student as well as his teacher has a personality and a life of his own to lead. This means at least seeing the pupil as a rational person, as opposed to an empty vessel to be filled up with the teacher's personal views or as wax to be moulded into a certain shape or pattern. The second is the cultivation of an awareness of the claims of the subject-matter. We have argued that the teacher has duties to the subject which he teaches. He has first of all a duty to teach it, as opposed to airing his own views on the contemporary political or social situation, and secondly he has a duty to teach it in a way which shows his respect for it and which engenders like respect for it in the pupils. To this end, he must strive for objectivity in his presentation of facts and conclusions. In some cases, however, the teacher may not know that he has distorted or coloured facts or made covert evaluations, for this can be done by tone of voice and presentation. To attempt to correct unconscious or unintentional bias of this kind it is not enough simply to strive for objectivity – a person may genuinely not know that his assessments are not objective. The teacher must therefore have a third kind of awareness, which can be characterized as self-awareness. He must ask himself if he is likely to distort the picture, if his tone of voice is such that it might lead people to think that he is contemptuous of a certain school of thought, if he is giving too much weight to a particular theory of his own, if his personality is such that what he intends as a casual remark is 'taken as gospel' by his pupils. If the teacher can cultivate these three kinds of awareness, the above dangers to the teaching relationship may be successfully avoided.

6 Private activity and public role

Just as the teacher can have private convictions which come into conflict with the duties of his official role, so he can lead a private life which people in general regard as unsuitable for a person with his public position. The question of how the teacher's private activity is related to his public role is not entirely distinct from the question of how his private views are related to it, for the teacher's private activity may exemplify the same private views which impinge on his role-performance. Thus the teacher with left-wing views may both preach left-wing politics in school and take part in demonstrations in private life. But we shall, for the purposes of examination, treat these two questions separately, and in this section concentrate on the relevance of private out-of-school activity to public role. Is a teacher unfitted for holding an official role by virtue of leading a private or personal life of which people disapprove?

We commonly find one of two extreme views on this question. One is to the effect that there is a continuity or solidarity between the actions or views which characterize a person in his private life and those which characterize him in his public life. On this view, if a teacher does something wrong or thought to be wrong in his private life, we have good grounds for excluding him from teaching posts. The other extreme view is that private life has no possible relevance to suitability for public office; the fact that a teacher beats his wife or commits adultery is entirely his own affair, and has nothing at all to do with his public position. Our argument will be that neither of these two extreme views will do on its own as an account of the relationship between private life and public role, the reason being that neither of them distinguishes different kinds of 'private activity of which people disapprove', which it is necessary to do before any balanced account can be given. In the first place, 'private life of which people disapprove' can refer to the sexual activities of a teacher: he may be leading an adulterous life, etc. Secondly, the activities may have nothing to do with sexual morals, but nevertheless be regarded as immoral by a number of people – e.g. drug-taking, insobriety, etc. Thirdly, a teacher may engage in political activities such as sit-ins and demonstrations of which people disapprove. Finally, he may have certain defects of character which are disapproved of: he may for example be mean, unpunctual, dishonest, self-centred, opinionated.

We have said that it is necessary to distinguish the various kinds of private activity before a balanced account can be given of its relevance to public role. It might be thought to be the case that one extreme thesis about the relationship between private activity and public role applies to some kinds of private activity, and the other extreme thesis to other kinds. Thus it might be argued that sexual morality is of relevance to suitability for a teaching position, whereas by and large 'defects of character' are not. Let us begin by examining this thesis about sexual morality. Three main arguments (apart from those with premises derived from religious belief) may be used to assert a general relevance of sexual morality to the role of the teacher.

The first is that, whatever may be true of some jobs, in the case of teaching there is a genuine possibility that sexual practices will be carried over from private to public life. Teachers are dealing with young people at an impressionable age, and to any teacher who is prone to sexual 'vice' impressionable young persons present a standing temptation. We are not disputing that it is a serious matter for a teacher to be guilty of actual misconduct with a pupil. Our question is rather whether the sexual 'vice' of a teacher in an *out-of-school* context ought to be any impediment to his employment in a school. There seems to be no general justification for this, but it can be said that different kinds of sexual 'vice' must be distinguished before a conclusion can be reached. For example, it might be argued that whereas fornication or adultery with another consenting adult is not of relevance to his official position, indulgence of homosexual impulses involving young boys *is* relevant. (This is not to say that homosexual relationships are *per se* relevant, but only that certain kinds might be said to be.) In such cases it could be said that it is irresponsible to take the attitude that one should wait and see whether any misconduct does occur, and if it does, then take action, given the effect that such misconduct may have on a pupil and given that the teacher may not be able fully to control his tendency.

The second argument used to back up the claim that sexual morality is relevant to public office is the argument from public example. The argument here is that the teacher, whether he likes it or not, is a public figure in the way in which a businessman, say, is not, and as a public figure he must set an example of high moral conduct. Hence his private life is relevant to his public life; or, to put it more strongly, in the case of a teacher, as in that of a minister of religion, there is no valid distinction between public and private life. Once again, there is a grain of truth in this argument. Teachers, like pop stars, do affect the behaviour and beliefs of young people over a wide area of their lives and there is therefore a duty for teachers (if not for pop stars) to avoid becoming notorious. But the further conclusion, that they should avoid the conduct altogether, follows only if we add an additional premise: that the private lives of teachers will actually be investigated and exposed to public scrutiny. Now such scrutiny is most undesirable, but at the same time it is a fact that in some cases (e.g. in a village or small town) it is impossible for a teacher to keep his private life to himself, and in these situations the argument from public example has a good deal of force.

The third argument used to back up the claim that private sexual morality is relevant to public role is the argument from public co-operation: since successful teaching depends partly on the co-operation of parents, the teacher will not be able to carry out his role so well if he is known to pursue activities of which a large number of people disapprove. Unlike the arguments from the possibility of carry-over and from public example, this argument does not depend on an assumption that the private conduct actually *is* vicious, as distinct from being widely regarded as such. But like the argument from example, it applies only in situations where the teacher's conduct is likely to become generally known.

The second kind of private activity which we distinguished was activity such as drug-taking, insobriety, etc. If a teacher is known to take drugs or to be prone to indulge in excess of alcohol, does this render him unsuitable for his public role? As before, there are three possible arguments which might be used to support the affirmative position. The first is that such activities are likely to have a deleterious effect on the person's ability to teach. But such a statement requires empirical verification. If drug-taking and insobriety do affect a teacher's ability, then this is no longer a matter of private activity but of professional competence, and the teacher will be open to such sanctions as are brought to bear on the professionally incompetent. The second and third arguments are again those from public example and public co-operation. Again they apply only if the teacher's conduct is likely to become known, but it should be noted that since some forms of drug-taking are illegal this private activity is particularly liable to be dragged into the limelight by police investigation. On the other hand, it might be argued that it is positively useful for a teacher to drink and take drugs; given that a number of pupils undoubtedly do indulge in drug-taking and drinking, a teacher who has experienced these kinds of activity can better help pupils who may have problems as a result of such activities. This may well be the case, but one cannot on the basis of this recommend that teachers *ought* to indulge in such activities. A teacher is not a sociologist or a field-worker.

The third kind of activity in which a teacher may take part in private life may be referred to as political or social activity, such as attendance at sit-ins and demonstrations. This kind of activity raises somewhat different problems from the two foregoing, arising from two important differences it possesses: it is normally seen by the participants as a duty, not merely as permissible or desirable; and it is often essentially public and even publicity-seeking behaviour, though not in the sense of being part of his public role. Because of the latter feature, the teacher's political activity cannot be kept secret and so it might seem that the arguments from public example and public co-operation have maximum force. But in fact it is not the case, or at least the teacher himself logically cannot see it in this light. He will think that since he is doing his duty as a citizen he must be setting a *good*, not a bad, example, and any loss of parental co-operation resulting from his action must be balanced against the claims of his political beliefs. It is therefore the task of *others* to decide whether a teacher's political activities are a bar to his employment. In so doing they need to take into account, not chiefly the content of his creed, but how far they think his type of political behaviour is a good example to pupils, how far parents do object to given views, how far they are capable of respecting honest conviction and enthusiasm even where they do not share the views. These are difficult issues. But it should be noted that since the teacher's behaviour in this sphere can affect his teaching in ways which other forms of private behaviour escape, he cannot claim that his political private life is his own affair.

The fourth kind of private activity was that involving defects of character, such as dishonesty, unpunctuality, self-opinionatedness, meanness, etc. Now a character-trait, good or bad, is a disposition to act in certain very general types of circumstances in certain ways defined by the trait in question; so the question whether defects in private conduct are relevant to fitness for a school post depends partly on whether the circumstances in which the trait is manifested obtain in school life as well as in private life. Such is the all-inclusiveness of school life, however, that it is difficult to think of *any* trait that might not on occasion be shown in school. On the other hand, it does not follow that no one with any defects of character is fit for a teacher's role; for since everyone has some defects of character, this would lead to the conclusion that no one is fit to be a teacher. The point must be put in terms of the degree and kind of defect: a person is, other things being equal, unsuited to be a teacher if he possesses to a considerable degree a defect of a kind which is bound to be manifested in any corporate endeavour (such as dishonesty) or bound to be manifested in teaching in particular, such as lack of patience, inability to keep his temper, lack of sympathy, self-centredness. The relevance of sympathy will be discussed more fully in our next chapter, and that of patience and even-temperedness is fairly obvious. But a word is needed about self-centredness, which is perhaps a less obvious candidate for a relevant defect.

There are three ways in which self-centredness may affect the public role of the teacher. The first is that the teacher may constantly refer to himself and his own doings. This kind of self-centredness may be called the egoism of self-reference. Within limits, of course, there is nothing wrong with this – indeed, we shall argue in the next chapter that it is desirable – but when it is overdone it may cause embarrassment and loss of respect, and so interfere with teaching duties. The second kind of self-centredness is the egoism of self-opinion. This defect leads teachers to obtrude their own private views in the way discussed earlier, though selfless devotion to a cause can have the same effect. Closely connected is the third kind of self-centredness, the egoism of self-absorption. In this third kind the teacher is concerned, whatever he is teaching or talking about, with the fact that *he* is doing it, and doing it in his own way. The emphasis in this case, we might say, is not on 'the teaching of the subject, as it happens, by me', but rather on 'my-teaching-of-the-subject'. The view here is that there is only one legitimate way to teach a subject or only one legitimate point of view on the subject – the teacher's own. This failing is found particularly in heads of departments. What is wrong with it is that it diverts attention from the subject to the person teaching it and to his way of teaching it.

The antidotes to these three kinds of egoism consist in the techniques mentioned in connexion with the obtruding of private views: the cultivation of awareness that pupils as well as teachers have personalities and lives of their own to lead, and that the subject-matter exerts certain claims. As before, the teacher must also cultivate self-awareness, and ask himself if he is all too likely to be absorbed in his own doings and his own theories. If these three kinds of awareness can be cultivated, the *malaise* of egoism can to a great extent be overcome.

7 Conclusion

We have argued that 'teacher' is a role-job, where 'role' is defined in terms of a set of determining rights and duties. The determining rights and duties of the teacher are of two kinds, contractual and implicational. Contractual determining rights and duties belong to the teacher by virtue of his contract of employment, and are held against and owed to the employer. Implicational determining rights and duties are those rights and duties which any person who is a teacher will have, simply in virtue of the aims of teaching. These rights are held by the teacher against the pupils, their parents and society, and the duties are owed by the teacher to the pupils, to the subject-matter and to society.

We have further maintained that the teacher may, in the pursuit of his duties, select material for study and attempt to inculcate knowledge, claiming that this is for the good of the pupils. We have suggested that consultation with pupils on teaching methods, curricula and formulation of rules can be not only valuable aids to the mental development of pupils but also part of their rights. But we have cast doubt on the desirability of pupil participation in disciplinary matters.

As well as having certain determining rights and duties which accrue to him because he acts in a social role, the individual teacher will have certain personal beliefs and convictions, which may come into conflict with what he is required to do in his capacity as role-occupant. We have argued that neither the 'ignore-your-own-attitude' view nor the 'resign-if-you-disagree' view can be accepted without qualification as the means of resolving the conflict between public duty and private conscience. We have indicated how the teacher may use the teaching situation, wittingly or unwittingly, as a vehicle for his private views, and we have suggested that this distortion of the teaching situation can be avoided if the teacher cultivates self-awareness and awareness of the pupils as persons and of the claims of the subject-matter.

In cases where a teacher indulges in private activities of which the majority of people in society disapprove, we have claimed that there is no general relevance of private activity to fitness for public position. Distinctions must be drawn between different kinds of private activity, some of which may be relevant to fitness for public position and others not.

Chapter Six

The teacher and personal relationships

It is often said that teaching has a special status among jobs in that it is especially *personal*. It is also claimed that teachers should (or that they should not) have personal relationships with their pupils, and pupils often complain that the attitude of their teachers is too impersonal. In this final chapter we shall investigate the notion of personal relationships, and consider how far and in what sense the teacher can and should have personal relationships with his pupils.

1 Relationships and attitudes

We can use the word 'relationship' in two ways: to stand for the situation, bond or occasion which links two or more people, or to stand for the attitudes which people so linked have to each other. As examples of the first kind of relationship we might mention kinship, marriage, business association, meeting through contingencies or emergencies, etc. As examples of the second kind we might mention fear, pride, respect, envy, contempt, etc. Thus someone seeing an adult with a child might ask 'What is the relationship between that pair?' and receive an answer in terms of the first kind of relationship: 'teacher and pupil', 'father and son', etc. Or he might ask 'What sort of relationship do Jones and his son have?' and receive an answer in terms of the second kind of relationship:

'Jones has a great affection for his son but his son has nothing but contempt for him'.

The two kinds of relationship are connected in various complex ways. For example, if the situation is a business transaction then the attitude of the parties would not characteristically be one of, say, affection, although there is no logical impediment to such an attitude developing out of the business transactions. Again, if people in one situation develop certain attitudes towards each other then new situations may develop out of the attitudes, and marriage is only the most obvious of the many possible cases of this. Nevertheless, although sometimes the effect of one factor will be to determine positively or negatively the nature of the other, many different permutations and combinations are possible. For example, the situation of kinship is compatible with a large number of possible attitudes, and the same may well be true of the teacher–pupil situation.

We have in effect described the nature of the teacher–pupil situation in previous chapters, and come to the conclusions that it is a role-relationship of a particular kind. Let us now turn therefore, to a consideration of teacher–pupil relationships in the *attitude* sense of the term. (In this chapter we shall mean this sense when we talk of teacher–pupil relationships, unless we specify the situation sense.) We shall begin with a brief consideration of attitudes in general. What is an attitude?

The first important point to make about attitudes is that they are two-sided. In the first place, attitudes must be *to* something: it is conceptually impossible for an attitude to lack an object. In the second place, attitudes must be *of* something, where 'something' stands for a disposition to feel and act in characteristic ways towards the object of the attitude. For example the attitude of fear held towards something disposes a person to avoid it, to feel distress if it is imminent and so on.

But an attitude is not merely a bundle of manifestations. It involves also a belief as to the nature of its object. Although the object of an attitude can always be described in various ways, for any particular attitude there will be one description under which the object of the attitude must by definition be thought to fall. For example, an attitude cannot logically be one of hope unless it is to an object which is believed to be in some sense a *good* to the hoper. The connexion between hope and an imagined good is thus a necessary one, and we might go as far as to say that a person could not understand the meaning of 'hope' unless he knew what it was to imagine a good. A similar analysis applies to all attitudes; they can be identified by means of the characteristics which their object is believed to possess. The object under the description which is implied by the attitude-name may be called the *formal object* of that attitude. For example, the formal object of hope is an imagined good which – it is believed – may come about, the formal object of fear is a believed danger, the formal object of pride something believed to be to the proud person's credit, the formal object of contempt something believed to be of no significance and so on.

The belief about the object on which a given attitude logically depends, which we shall term the formal-object belief, will of course depend in its turn on further beliefs. For example, a belief that toads are dangerous, which is logically involved in the attitude of fear towards toads, rests in its turn on beliefs such as that they are poisonous or that they spread disease. The connexion between the former, formal-object belief and the latter, factual beliefs is not, however, a logical one, like that between the beliefs and the attitudes. There are no particular factual beliefs about toads which someone who holds they are dangerous must logically have, because a formal-object belief is always partly evaluative: what we see as dangerous, creditable, demanding, etc., depends in the last resort on our views of good and evil. The factual beliefs, therefore, serve as *grounds* for the formal-object belief: good or bad grounds, according to whether or not they are true and, if true, sufficient to justify it.

It should be noted in passing that the question 'What is your attitude to . . .?' can be answered in three different ways: by naming one's attitude directly, by stating one's formal-object belief, or by stating some other belief which is held to give such obvious grounds for a particular attitude that the attitude itself need not be stated. Thus in answer to the question 'What is your attitude to the Headmaster?' a teacher might reply 'Contempt', or

'I regard him as of no significance at all', or 'I regard him as a fool' – and be expressing the same attitude in all three cases. The expression 'regard as' is often used, as here, to signify either a 'formal-object belief' – a belief logically implying the appropriateness of a particular attitude – or a belief which at least suggests that a particular attitude is appropriate.

Having given a brief outline of the nature of attitudes in general, we can go on to consider types of attitudes towards human beings, with a view to asking the question which of these are possible and desirable constituents of the relationship between teacher and pupil. For our purposes we can classify these attitudes with reference to three possible ways of looking at human beings. Firstly, they can be viewed as generic human selves or persons as such, in other words in terms of those features which make them persons or are 'the distinctive endowment of a human being' – the conception we discussed in Chapter Three. Attitudes of the first type, then, are those which are grounded in the belief that the human being in question possesses certain features simply *qua* human being. Secondly, human beings can be viewed as belonging to a certain general type or class of persons. For example, they can be described and seen in terms of their occupation – as a teacher, say – or in terms of some activity they perform – as a motorist, say – and there are many other such possibilities of grouping. Accordingly, the second type of attitude is grounded in beliefs about a person which are thought to apply to him in virtue of his membership of a given class. Thirdly, human beings can be viewed as 'idiosyncratic selves' or distinctive individuals. Viewed in this way they are regarded neither as 'persons as such' nor as 'persons of this kind' but rather as 'this particular person rather than that one'. The third type of attitude is grounded in beliefs about the nature of the idiosyncratic self in question.

Before we proceed to discuss these three basic types of attitudes and the features of human beings on which they depend it might prevent misunderstanding if we note several general points. First of all, the claim is not that there are three separate 'selves', but rather that one and the same person can be regarded in terms of these three basic types of attitude. Secondly, the types of attitude are not mutually exclusive: to think of a person as a teacher or motorist and to have attitudes to him as a result does not rule out, one would hope, regarding him at the same time as a person and as an individual. Thirdly, while it is doubtful whether it is psychologically possible to regard a person exclusively in terms of only one of the three types of attitude, there is no doubt that it is possible, and common, to view a person more in terms of one than another. For example, to the Good Samaritan[1] the man by the roadside was mainly 'a man in need of help', although idiosyncratic features would no doubt soon emerge as their relationship developed. Fourthly, many of the problems of morality can be shown to be connected with the balance between these three possible types of attitude. The first, as we shall see, is morally the most basic, but the complexities of the moral life as it affects personal relationships cannot be analyzed in terms of it alone.

Let us now look in more detail at the types of attitudes and those ways of regarding human beings on which they depend. We may begin with a brief reminder of the nature of the 'distinctive human endowment' which constitutes the generic human self. As we saw in Chapter Three, this endowment consists of *reason* in all its aspects: theoretical reason, and practical reason (or Kantian 'rational will') which manifests itself in self-determination and rule-following. We suggested that the emotions and desiring element can also be seen as having a rational aspect, since in man (as distinct from animals) they are based on discriminations made by the reason.

Before we can consider the kinds of attitudes which correspond to this way of looking at human beings, however, we must look briefly at a type of attitude to them which *rejects* the view of them which we have just outlined. We may call this type of attitude 'impersonal', in contrast to 'personal' attitudes which do regard human beings as persons.

[1] St Luke, X, vv. 30–35.

2 *Impersonal attitudes*

To see what is involved in regarding a human being in this impersonal way, consider the kind of attitudes we may have to animals. Of course, something very like a personal relationship can develop between a person and certain animals – dogs, monkeys, etc. But let us ignore this complication and take the example of the way in which a person might regard a badger or a crow. He might regard them aesthetically – as beautiful creatures – or causally, as complex conscious mechanisms. Now the important point for our purposes is that it is possible to regard a human being in this way. This can be illustrated in the type of attitude which a psychiatrist may have towards a patient who is mentally defective or otherwise suffering from some serious disorder. Let us suppose that the patient is abusive to the psychiatrist or offers violence. Now the good psychiatrist will show a type of attitude to this which can be described as 'impersonal'. His impersonality is that of the man with a purely technical problem to cope with. Just as a veterinary surgeon may try to remove a sharp object from an injured animal and be obliged to keep himself clear of the teeth or hooves of the animal, so the psychiatrist in the example will be doing what he can to help the patient but will be obliged to discount any abuse or violence which may be offered. Or, if he does not discount it, he will see it as further relevant data on which he may base his assessments of the patient's problems. In this sense, then, an 'impersonal' attitude is that of the efficient operator who manipulates a given object for one purpose or another and sees nothing personal in any reactions of his object. In the case of the psychiatrist the 'something' or 'object' may also be a human being. The important point may be put in other terms if we say that the object of the impersonal attitude in this sense is seen as being of such a kind that a sufficient causal explanation can be found for its behaviour.

What are we to say of impersonality in this sense? It is certainly an attitude which may be adopted not only by a psychiatrist but also by, say, a psychiatric social worker to some of his particularly difficult cases or by anyone dealing with the mentally impaired.

He will see them and their behaviour in causal terms. To see them in this way does not, of course, exclude the experiencing of certain emotions towards them, such as pity or sympathy of a sort. But it does exclude regarding them as persons in the full sense. For, without raising the problem of the freedom of the will, we can maintain that to see human action or speech in this way is to refuse to take it seriously, to refuse to see in it the significance which the agent sees or other people would normally see in it. Thus it is incompatible with attitudes such as resentment or disapproval, which presuppose that their object is a person who means what he says and does.[1] By contrast with this impersonal attitude, we have a *personal* attitude to someone if we see him as a person who acts in ways open to purposive explanation. We take seriously what he says and does and assume that his behaviour proceeds from rational policies and responsible decisions, and we see in his behaviour the significance which would normally be attached to it. In other words, we regard him as a self-determining and rule-following being: in short, a person. As we saw earlier, the notion of a person is itself evaluative, and to regard a human being as a person is to have some attitude to him which at the least acknowledges his significance as an autonomous agent.

Our contention is that a teacher–pupil relationship must be personal as opposed to impersonal in this fundamental sense. In other words, teacher and pupil must see each other as persons to be regarded as self-determining and rule-following beings. To insist on this point is simply to insist that education be *education*, and not conditioning. The point is worth insisting on, not only because there are current ideologies which blur the distinction, but also because there may be psychological theories of education the effect of which is the reduction of human action to the category of causal process. The point is not that teachers are encouraged by such theories or ideologies to be harsh or repressive; the reverse may be true. It is simply that such theories undermine the status of human beings as self-determining and rule-following beings.

[1] See P. F. Strawson, 'Freedom and Resentment', *Proceedings of the British Academy*, 1962; R. S. Downie, 'Objective and Reactive Attitudes,' *Analysis*, 1966.

Having made this point in sweeping terms we must now qualify it in an important respect. Account must be taken of the age and psychological nature of the pupil. Clearly, some behaviour of some children ought to be seen in causal rather than in purposive terms. There are disturbed and maladjusted children, and towards them it may be more fitting to adopt the impersonal attitude which a psychiatrist may have for a patient. And even normal children (and indeed adults) will manifest behaviour for which causal rather than purposive categories are more appropriate. No doubt it is often a problem to decide when such an impersonal attitude is appropriate, but it would be entirely unrealistic to deny that sometimes with some pupils, old or young, it is appropriate. But despite the important qualification it is essential that the attitude of teacher and pupil towards each other should be one showing awareness that each is a self-determining and rule-following being.

It should be noted that in saying teacher–pupil relationships must be personal in this sense we are making both a factual and a moral claim. The factual claim is that our account of human nature, in terms of a personhood which cannot be reduced to a bundle of causal processes, is broadly true; a corollary of this factual claim is that it is in general reasonable to adopt towards human beings the types of attitude which have the notion of a person as part of their formal object: approval and disapproval, gratitude and resentment, indignation and so on. The moral claim is that it is not merely reasonable but also morally right to adopt such attitudes rather than those of the psychiatrist, since personhood comprises what is valuable about a human being, and to ignore this endowment where it exists is not merely to mistake his nature but also to devalue him.

It might be objected here that talk of these personal attitudes as morally appropriate is unnecessary, on the ground that anyone who believes that human beings are in general possessed of rational will *cannot but* regard normal human beings as persons. But this is not so; it is very easy and tempting to escape from the strain of relationships by regarding even normal people as though they were things. For example, the teacher who greets a general complaint from pupils, not with an attempt to understand and assess the pupils' case, but simply by saying 'You're just excited before the holidays', or 'You're just tired after your exams', or 'You're just restless because you haven't been able to play football this week', is regarding them as causal mechanisms with no rationality of their own.

We suggest, then, that there is a type of attitude which is both logically appropriate to human beings viewed as persons and morally required in that we *ought* to regard human beings as persons rather than things. This type of attitude may be called personal in contrast to the impersonal attitude of the psychiatrist; it is sometimes also called *reactive*, as opposed to objective.[1]

But note that whereas reactiveness is necessary for moral appropriateness of attitude, it is not sufficient. There are many reactive attitudes which are not morally worthy. For example, if the teacher mentioned above reacts with unwarranted resentment to a justified complaint, he is certainly regarding his pupils as persons who are responsible for their conduct, taking their views seriously, and so on; but his attitude is nevertheless not the right one. The right attitude to human beings is one which accommodates the importance of the characteristic human endowment of reason, not merely by acknowledging its presence, but also by fostering its activity. Let us now consider the nature of this morally appropriate attitude. In analyzing it allowance must be made for the two main features making up rational will, and for the endowment of theoretical reason.

3 Respect

Kant provides an example in the *Groundwork* which hints at what is morally required in our attitude to self-determination. He takes the case of a man for whom things are going well but who sees others, whom he could help, struggling with hardships. Kant supposes that this man says to himself 'What does it matter to me? Let everyone be as happy as Heaven wills or as he can make himself; I won't deprive him of anything; I won't even envy him; only I have no wish to contribute anything to his well-being or to his

[1] Strawson, op. cit.

support in distress'.[1] Now Kant holds that such an attitude is not the worst possible, but he also holds that a will which decided to act in such a manner 'would be in conflict with itself, since many a situation might arise in which the man needed love and sympathy from others, and in which . . . he would rob himself of all hope of the help he wants'.[2] The point emerges more clearly when Kant discusses the same example again in another context. He writes that

> the natural end which all men seek is their own happiness. Now humanity could no doubt subsist if everybody contributed nothing to the happiness of others but at the same time refrained from deliberately impairing their happiness. This is, however, merely to agree negatively and not positively with humanity as an end in itself unless everyone endeavours also, so far as in him lies, to further the ends of others. For the ends of a subject who is an end in himself must, if this conception is to have its *full* effect in me, be also, as far as possible, *my* ends.[3]

Kant is here suggesting that we should treat the ends of others, their ends of inclination or what they pursue in the exercise of their self-determination, as if they were our own. If the morally appropriate attitude to self-determining agents involves positive concern for them of this nature it will involve what is best characterized by the concept of sympathy. But 'sympathy' can mean various things, and we shall have to qualify it to distinguish the relevant sense.

Professor W. G. Maclagan distinguishes three meanings of 'sympathy' (while admitting that other meanings may be possible).[4] The first he calls 'animal sympathy', by which he means a sort of 'psychological infection of one creature by another, as when panic fear spreads in a herd', and even in a human context there is 'in the operation of such animal sympathy, little or no sense of others as

[1] Kant, *The Fundamental Principles of the Metaphysic of Morals*, translated by H. J. Paton as *The Moral Law*, pp. 90–91 (London, Hutchinson's University Library, 1948).

[2] Kant, op. cit., p. 91.

[3] Kant, op. cit., p. 98.

[4] W. G. Maclagan, 'Respect For Persons As a Moral Principle', part I, section 8, *Philosophy*, 1960.

independent individual centres of experience. What we have is rather a sense of an indeterminate psychological atmosphere . . .' In the second place, there is what Maclagan terms 'passive sympathy' or 'empathy'. This is sympathy in a distinctively human mode because, while there may be no clear line between it and animal sympathy, passive sympathy does involve consciousness of others as experiencing subjects. It is a matter of 'feeling oneself into the experience of the other' or of an emotional 'identification of ourself with the other'. The third form of sympathy, which Maclagan distinguishes as 'active sympathy', is the 'sympathy of practical *concern for* others as distinguished from simply *feeling with* them'. Now sympathy in the third of Maclagan's senses is the concept we require to analyze the example which Kant provided of a man who did not help others in pursuing their ends of inclination. Such a man did not show respect for persons as ends, and he did not do so because his conduct lacked the concern for others expressed in the concept of 'active sympathy'. We must therefore make room for this concept in our account of the morally appropriate attitude towards persons conceived generically as rational wills.

We argued that people are not only self-determining but also rule-following. The question which now arises concerns the attitudinal component which is morally appropriate towards persons conceived as rule-following creatures.[1] If in general we can characterize the attitude morally appropriate to persons as self-determining agents as one of sympathy, we can characterize the morally appropriate attitude to persons as rule-following (clumsily perhaps) as one of *rule-awareness*. What is involved in rule-awareness?

First of all, rule-awareness involves the realization that the existence of rules sets permissible limits to the exercise of sympathy, or, in other words, that the impersonal nature of rules qualifies the personal concern involved in the exercise of sympathy. Let us consider the point in terms of a dramatic but perhaps not unrealistic type of example. Suppose that a teacher is aware of the difficult home circumstances of a certain pupil and has been showing sympathy towards the pupil. But suppose that in the course of this

[1] See R. S. Downie and Elizabeth Telfer, *Respect For Persons*, pp. 27–8 (London, Allen and Unwin, 1969).

the teacher becomes aware that the pupil is involved in some criminal activities. However much concern the teacher might have for the pupil he would be acting wrongly if he were to pretend that the criminal activities did not matter or if he were to tell lies about the activities on the pupil's behalf. *A fortiori* this is true of the relationship between two adults. If another adult has broken an acknowledged rule it is in an important sense patronizing to play this down on the grounds that one sympathizes with his purposes.

In the second place, rule-awareness involves the realization that other people have moral conceptions which may differ from one's own, and that there are limits beyond which it is not morally permissible to go in persuading them to act against these conceptions. We may attempt to argue them out of their views – sometimes, indeed, there is a duty to try, and sometimes even a duty to prevent someone from doing what he morally thinks he ought if we morally think that he ought not. But these are different cases from that in which one person attempts to undercut another's rational will in order to get him to do what he believes to be wrong. Suppose, for example, that a teenage pupil is refusing to help with the school dance because he thinks dancing is immoral. It is legitimate for teachers and fellow pupils to attempt to convince him by argument that he is mistaken – thereby running the risk that they will be the ones who change their minds! – but it is contrary to rule-awareness to attempt, by ridicule, bribery or threats, to persuade him to act against his convictions.[1]

The third important aspect of the distinctive human endowment was the *theoretical* reason. Now the morally appropriate attitude to this (which we can call 'regard for intellect') combines features of sympathy and rule-awareness. For the achievement of truth in their theoretical speculations is an end which most people have, and it is one which imposes rules of thought upon the thinker – not in this case rules which he creates, but objective rules which he comes, partly through education, to adopt as his own. To have regard for another's intellect, then, is to take seriously his curiosity, to refrain from misleading him, to avoid overbearing him by specious argument, to be willing to take his arguments seriously

[1] See W. G. Maclagan, 'How Important Is Moral Goodness?', *Mind*, *1955*.

and acknowledge the possibility that he may be right, to refrain from pretending to agree when he says something one thinks fallacious and so on – in short, to acknowledge him as in some sense a fellow-intellectual. As we have suggested, regard for intellect is not in the end an attitude separable from sympathy and rule-awareness; but it is so important as an aspect of the teacher's correct attitude to pupils, and of the more educated person's correct attitude to the less well educated, that it merits a special mention of its own.

If we are correct in analyzing the generic human self in terms of the concept of reason, in turn regarded as the ability of human beings to theorize, to be self-determining and to be rule-following, then we have grounds for saying that the morally appropriate attitude is one of sympathy, rule-awareness and regard for intellect. It is helpful to characterize this attitude as being one of respect for persons as ends. The idea of respect for persons as ends is, of course, a Kantian one, although our treatment of it here is not strictly Kantian. Kant regarded one of the *a priori* principles which govern all morally permissible behaviour or, as he sometimes puts it, one of the formulations of the Categorical Imperative, as being 'Act so as to treat humanity, whether in your own person or in that of another, never only as a means but always also as an end.'[1] Our treatment of this important idea differs in some significant ways from that of Kant – particularly over the emphasis which we lay on sympathy – but nevertheless we regard Kant as expressing, in the form of a principle, the nature of the attitude which is morally appropriate to human beings conceived as 'generic selves'.

This moral relationship between people conceived as generic selves is the most fundamental human relationship, firstly in the sense that any contingent occasion can provide a situation in which it can be shown, and secondly in the sense that it is implicit in, and places morally permissible limits on, all other types of human relationship. Elaboration of the second point will need to wait till we have discussed other types of relationships, but a few examples will be sufficient to clarify the first point. The best known example of the first point is that provided by the parable of the

[1] Kant, op. cit., p. 96.

Good Samaritan.[1] The man who had been attacked by robbers and was lying by the wayside was ignored by two passers-by, who had their own reasons for ignoring him. The Good Samaritan, however, responded to the idea that here was another human being who needed help. In other words, he displayed in his actions that active sympathy which we have claimed to be an essential component in the attitude of respect for persons as self-determining creatures. The contingency of the attack brought the two men into a basic human situation in which the Samaritan showed the morally appropriate attitude.

Respect for persons also involved rule-awareness, and people are frequently in a situation where they are required to show this. There are genuine differences of opinion in contemporary society as to what rules are morally permissible or mandatory, and such differences are often aired in discussion and witnessed in practice. The process of mutual adjustment which these differences require is the manifestation of a relationship of respect for one another as rule-following creatures. This kind of respect falls under the notion of *tolerance*, and the fact that tolerance is regarded widely as a basic value of our society indicates our belief in the fundamental nature of respect for persons as rule-following creatures.

It goes without saying that teachers and pupils, like any other persons, should have to each other an attitude of respect for persons, constituting part of their relationship to each other within their role-situation. But it is also a familiar feature of school life that this relationship often does not exist. For example, teachers and pupils often treat each other with a rudeness that they would never show to anyone else, as though ordinary considerations about sympathy were waived in this relationship. (We are not of course talking about justified reproof when we speak of the teacher's rudeness, but of the gibe about personal appearance or sarcasm about home circumstances to which teachers too often resort in dealing with pupils.) We have here a second sense in which the relationship between teacher and pupil should be personal: that of 'involving normal respect for each other as persons'. This sense goes beyond the sense isolated earlier, 'regarding each other as persons rather than things'.

[1] St Luke X. vv. 30–35.

Note that respect for persons is in itself personal in a third sense: it takes account of individual differences. For in making a person's ends one's own one has to take account of what his particular ends happen to be; and whereas some ends, such as freedom from pain, may be said to be universal, others vary from person to person. Again, in showing rule-awareness with regard to a particular person, we have to take account of what his particular convictions are. Thus it might be said that whereas the object of the attitude of respect is the generic self the way in which the attitude manifests itself will vary in accordance with the nature of the individual in question. But this feature of respect does not make it an attitude directed towards what we earlier called the idiosyncratic self. For as we said earlier, attitudes directed to the idiosyncratic self are concerned with this person rather than that one – they are what we may call 'exclusive' – whereas respect is concerned equally with all individuals.

An objection might be raised to the claim that the attitude of respect so conceived is the fundamental attitude in human relationships. If 'fundamental' means 'morally fundamental', then it must be possible to adopt the attitude at will (for anything morally required must be open to choice), but this attitude, it might be argued, is not under the control of the will. In dealing with this objection we shall accept the assumed premise – that anything morally required must be open to choice – and concentrate on the main substance of the objection. There seem in fact to be two ways of interpreting the objection, a more and a less radical way. Let us begin with the more radical way.

The more radical objection is to the effect that attitudes as such, not just this particular attitude, cannot be adopted at will. Attitudes, it might be maintained, grow up gradually as a result of education or social conditioning and cannot be commanded. In reply, there is no need to deny that attitudes do develop as a result of education and social conditioning. The important point for the present is that they also develop as the result of acting in terms of *principles*. What is the relationship between a principle and an attitude?

There are two connexions, one logical and one causal. There is a logical connexion in that if a person has a certain attitude towards something he will necessarily adopt certain principles of action towards it *other things being equal*, and the general nature of the principles can be inferred from knowledge of the attitude. We need to add the qualification in order to allow for conflicting attitudes. Thus, if a man has an attitude of fear towards cows, he will (other things being equal) adopt a principle of avoiding cows; but if he has another attitude which is one of humiliation and self-loathing towards the first attitude, he may well make it a principle to walk through fields of cows as often as he can, hoping to cure himself. We can make this point in another way by saying that certain principles of action are logically connected with certain attitudes insofar as these attitudes can be regarded as working in isolation.

As can be seen in the example of the man's attitude towards cows, the connexion between an attitude and a principle can also be causal. For, even although a person does not have a certain attitude, if he consistently acts on a certain principle he may find he has acquired the attitude; to act *as if* one had a certain attitude may be the first step, and a necessary one, in acquiring the attitude. Assuming, then, that we can act on a principle, we can also develop in ourselves attitudes.

At this point it might be objected that, whatever may now be conceded about the general possibility of developing attitudes in oneself through principles of action, the specific attitude of respect does not lend itself to this treatment because an essential component in the attitude of respect has been said to be sympathy, and sympathy is a gift of nature; some people have a sympathetic disposition, while others do not. This, of course, is the less radical interpretation of the objection.

The answer is first of all to assert that sympathy, or at least the germ of sympathy, is something which is part of the natural endowment of all normal human beings. The ability to share in and respond to the feelings of others is a part of the human biological inheritance. In the second place, we can say, utilizing the argument produced in reply to the more radical objection, that if a man possesses the raw material of an attitude, in the form of some measure of the appropriate feelings, he can develop it by acting appropriately; and whereas the strength of an attitude may not always be under the direct control of a man's will, it is always possible for him to adopt the principle of action which will develop the germs of activity which (we hold) everyone possesses, and thus strengthen his moral attitude.

Our conclusions so far are that teachers and pupils, inasmuch as they are persons, ought to have a relationship to each other which is personal in three senses: it is reactive rather than objective, acknowledging the fact that the parties to it are persons and not things; it is respectful of persons, i.e. cherishing and fostering this personhood; and it is (by virtue of the nature of respect) individualistic rather than anti-individualistic, taking account of some of the particular features of the parties involved. It is possible for every individual to develop those attitudes to others in which this relationship consists.

4 Persons as 'types'

It may be objected to the foregoing analysis that teacher and pupil are not two moral agents in a vacuum, with only their 'personhood' to characterize them. They also belong to the categories of teacher and pupil respectively and will be regarded by each other as such – in other words, as 'types'. Such a way of looking at people, it might be maintained, must after all be impersonal in some sense; and if it is inevitable in their situation, as it might seem to be, we cannot after all maintain that teacher–pupil relationships should be personal.

Before we consider this objection we must make some clarificatory points. The first of these is that simply to look at people as falling into various categories need not involve any attitudes at all; it may amount to nothing but recognition of obvious facts. The second point is an equally obvious one: the adoption of any attitude involves a form of categorization. For to form a formal-object belief about a person, for example that he is dangerous, is in effect to put him in a category, that of dangerous people. Moreover, a person may be put into a formal-object category on grounds of belonging to another category; thus to categorize someone as a fascist may be to provide grounds good or bad for categorizing him as dangerous. The third and most important point is that categorizing in general must be distinguished from what we shall call *pigeonholing*: the assumption that nothing about a person is of significance except the category into which he has been placed. Pigeonholing is not merely the basis for attitudes, but itself embodies a kind of attitude, or rather the denial of one: denial that the person pigeonholed has any importance as an individual. Pigeonholing is of course a question of degree; we may over-emphasize the category into which we put someone without altogether losing sight of his individuality.

In the light of these remarks, let us go back to the objection with which this section began, and consider whether categorizing people as teachers, or pupils, or in any other way is indeed *impersonal*, in any of the senses summed up at the end of the previous section. The first sense was 'objective' or 'regarding the object as subject to causal laws'. Now it is clear that categorizing in general need not involve this kind of impersonality. We do of course employ particular categories, such as 'not responsible' or 'schizophrenic', which mark off the formal-object belief or the possible grounds of an objective attitude; where these categories are correctly applied, we are justified in adopting such an attitude. We might note also that one form of extreme pigeonholing involves an objective attitude: that form which embodies an assumption that people in a certain category are completely predictable and inevitably act in a certain fashion. Thus a teacher might pigeonhole a boy as a teenager who is 'bound to' act in certain ways typical of teenagers. In doing this he is denying the boy any purposes of his own. But to think of someone as a teenager clearly need not, and usually does not, involve a belief that he is *bound* to act in certain ways.

The second sense of 'impersonal' was 'lacking respect for persons'. It cannot be contrary to respect for persons simply to see that various general things can be said about groups of them. Nor can we give any *general* answer to the question whether it is contrary to respect for persons to form those categories on which we base our attitudes. Such a question asks in effect whether it is immoral to form attitudes to people, and the only general answer possible seems to be the vacuous one that there are some attitudes which it is immoral to adopt on some grounds. What *can* be said however is that some categorization, so far from being inimical to respect, is positively implied in it. For example, the sympathy aspect of respect implies recognition of categories such as 'those in trouble', 'those in need', etc., and the rule-awareness aspect implies the recognition of moral categories such as 'dishonest', 'lazy', etc. It is also clear that pigeonholing, as opposed to categorizing in general, is contrary to respect for persons; for it implies that the individuality of the pigeonholed person does not matter, that he is *nothing but* a teenager, or lazy, or delinquent, or intelligent, or whatever, and what pertains to his pigeonhole is the only significant thing about him. In other words, pigeonholing goes against the individualized aspect of respect for persons: it is impersonal in the third sense of the personal/impersonal distinction.

It might be objected that since any categorizing must be based on likenesses rather than differences it must always be impersonal in this third sense, even if not in the first two senses. But though the premise is of course true, the conclusion embodies a confusion between categorizing and pigeonholing. It is perfectly possible to categorize someone as dishonest, and disapprove of him accordingly, while recognizing differences between him and other dishonest people. A teacher may say to himself 'Smith and Jones are both dishonest, but Smith is lazy as well, whereas Jones is industrious', or 'Smith and Jones are both dishonest, but Smith is set a bad example at home, whereas Jones has no excuse'. Only if the teacher says 'Smith and Jones are a pair of liars and that's all there is to to be said about them' is he being impersonal in the third sense – but then he is clearly pigeonholing rather than categorizing.

We can amplify and illustrate these points by connecting them with the four senses of 'role' distinguished in the previous chapter; for to see a person as a role-incumbent, in any of the senses of 'role', is to categorize him in some way. The first sense of 'role' is simply the class into which people fall in virtue of some property they have in common. The notion of a role in this sense introduces no new points, as it is in effect equivalent to a category; hence the same conclusions can be drawn about roles in this sense and personal relationships as were drawn about categories.

The second sense of 'role' is that of function in a social system. Now at first sight it might seem that to see a person as playing a role in this sense is the basis of adopting an objective attitude to him, in somewhat the same way that seeing a person as schizophrenic is the basis of an objective attitude; for the use of the term 'role' in this sense is by analogy with its use in biology and mechanics, in functional explanations of the existence of parts of animate organisms and of machines. But the analogy need not be pressed so far. A person can be seen as performing a function, in that his group contributes causally to some socially significant end within the social system, without any implication that he himself is a causally determined cog in the social machine. For example, that familiar group, classroom comedians, may be seen as performing the function of 'releasers of tension', thus enabling the emotional equilibrium of the class to be maintained. But to say this is not to say that they are in some way causally determined to act as they do; indeed, the sophisticated pupil may not only deliberately choose to play the fool, but even do so *in order* to lower the emotional temperature.

Of course, it is possible to regard the society in question (the class in this case) as an organism which in some mysterious way *develops* or *produces* people to fulfil such functions; this way of thinking does embody an objective attitude to people, who are seen as mere organs. But it is more plausible to regard the talk of function as merely a metaphor – a way of describing the useful effects someone's behaviour in fact has on the society *as if* he were an organ of it. Even on this metaphorical interpretation, thinking of people in terms of their function has its dangers: it may lead the thinker to *value* people simply in terms of what they as a group do for society, and this is an example of the pigeonholing which, as we saw, is contrary to respect for persons.

The third way in which people can be seen as 'types' is as the incumbents of a set of rights and duties. Thus teacher and pupil can be seen, and can see each other, as the possessors of those rights and duties to each other which we discussed in our previous chapter. Now insofar as they are in a duty-situation with regard to each other, they can be said to have a certain kind of relationship which we may call 'official' or 'institutional' or again 'impersonal'. But note that this is a relationship in the situation sense of that word: it explains what the 'set-up' is which links teacher and pupil, but says nothing about the attitudes which they have to each other within this situation. To say that the teacher–pupil relationship, *qua* duty-relationship, is impersonal is to contrast it with such relationships as friendships and love affairs, not to say anything about attitudes. We shall consider in the next section how far role-relationships are compatible with personal relationships in the situation sense.

It might be said, however, that whereas *being* in a duty-situation implies nothing about attitudes, *seeing* each other as owed rights and owing duties does imply one particular – and, in view of our previous chapter, a morally appropriate – attitude to the duty-situation. This duty-attitude can be contrasted with other possible attitudes: for example, that of teachers and pupils who see each other merely as nuisances towards whom it is on balance prudent to behave as society requires.

This claim is certainly true, in a minimal sense at least. Indeed, we can characterize the attitudes embodied in the acknowledgment of reciprocal rights and duties in terms of our earlier distinctions between different kinds of personal and impersonal attitudes. To see someone as having a special duty to oneself – which only a responsible being can be said to have – is to take up a reactive attitude to him and moreover to respect him as a rule-following being. To see him as having special rights against oneself is an aspect of sympathy for him, of making his ends one's own in the context of an institutional framework. In seeing each other as parties to a role-relationship, then, teacher and pupil necessarily have to that extent an attitude to each other which is personal in the first two senses.

It is not immediately clear, however, that personalness in the third sense forms a necessary part of the acknowledgement of reciprocal rights and duties. For example, it might be said that since rights and duties suggest *rules*, they carry them with the notion that everyone falling under the rule should be treated in the same way. Now if a teacher could see his job in terms of a rigid application of rules then his attitude would be impersonal in the third sense. But whereas this view might make sense with regard to some roles (that of handing out some undifferentiated welfare allowance, or of collecting rents for an unbending landlord, for example) it does not fit the teacher's position because of the individualized nature of his duties. For example, one of his duties to his pupils is the general duty to impart knowledge to them. But part of this duty is to consider how best to cater for the differences in aptitude and inclination which individual pupils possess.

It is important that teacher and pupil should not only carry out their respective duties with due regard for individual differences, but also realize that they are dealing with individuals who have an existence apart from their roles. 'Role' in the rights-and-duties sense is a concept of social description and it is a useful tool for grouping duties, revealing structure in apparently unconnected activities and identifying various forms of social pressure. But this must not lead us to ignore the fact that it is *people* who perform the duties, pursue the activities and experience the pressures. If the idea of a pure ego is an abstraction, so is that of a role which is enacted without leaving the imprint of the person who is in the role. Hence, even if it is conceded that we never meet a person who is not in a role, this in no way suggests that it is not really a person whom we meet. Indeed, a common moral failing is to attend too much to a person's social role and not enough to the fact of his being a person; to have contempt for him because he is the school cleaner or over-deference towards him because he is the headmaster. Along these lines lies the sort of 'respect for persons' which is a vice, corrected, or over-corrected, by being 'no respecter of persons'.

It might be objected that our insistence on the individualized nature of the teacher's duty-attitude is inconsistent with a requirement which all role-incumbents have to meet with regard to those with whom they have to deal in their role: that of *impartiality*. Surely, it may be said, impartiality means treating everyone alike; if the teacher has to be impartial, he must after all have an attitude to his pupils which is impersonal in the third sense.

Now it is true that the teacher ought to be impartial. But this objection mistakes the nature of impartiality, which means not the ignoring of individual differences but the ignoring of those differences which are irrelevant to the nature of one's duties. For example, the impartial teacher marking an examination certainly does not treat everyone alike, but he differentiates performances by their merit, or in terms of effort shown, or (conceivably) as a means of encouragement or deflation, *not* according to the attractiveness or social standing of the pupils. Indeed, impartiality is often what is really meant when people say that a teacher should have an impersonal attitude to his pupils. We have therefore a fourth sense of the 'personal' and 'impersonal' distinction. In this sense, unlike the others, the teacher, *qua* role-incumbent, morally should have an *impersonal* rather than a personal attitude – but this impersonalness is of course hard to achieve.

The fourth way in which we can see people as types is to regard them as *playing* the role of an *x* or *y*, by analogy with playing a part in drama. Note that this goes beyond simply *having* the role of *x* or *y*, whether in the category, the function or the rights-and-duties sense of 'role'. To play a role is to sink oneself in a self-consistent all-embracing life-style. This fourth way of seeing people as types is especially significant as a *self*-directed attitude – a way of looking at oneself. We shall concentrate on this aspect, which in any case affects relationships with others, as we shall see.

In this sense of role, it is common for students to play at being students, for professors to play at being professors and so on. This idea is involved in what has come to be called 'projecting an image'. To 'project an image' is self-consciously to adopt a style of behaviour and hope to be identified with this style. 'Style of behaviour' must here be taken to include modes of speech, dress and general mannerisms. Sometimes these may be modelled on prominent people – 'pop stars', student leaders or the like. At other times the content of the role is made up of some ideal – what an ideal teacher or social worker or army officer ought to be like. The playing of a role in this sense is common in most occupations and social classes. An indication of this is that it is often possible to make a rough guess at people's occupations from the clothes they wear, their type of conversation and so on. Of course, factors other than role-playing are involved here, but it is undoubtedly true that role-playing is a fact of social life.

We can however distinguish various possibilities, of differing moral worth, within role-playing. Consider first that kind of acting whereby the teacher who on some occasion does not in fact feel particularly concerned about his pupils' troubles or interested in their progress acts as though he does. This kind of acting – which is surely part of every teacher's experience – is confined to the sphere of the role's demands, whether determining or accessory, and is one example of the process mentioned earlier, whereby a moral agent attempts to acquire the right attitude by acting as though he already had it. A second kind of role-playing is the process of forming and following an ideal as to how a member of a trade or profession ought to behave. For example, a teacher might form an ideal of the true or dedicated teacher, based on an actual teacher he had known or an amalgam of several or on a set of qualities. Whatever the causal origins of the ideal, one can easily imagine this being done and a person acting as he thinks the ideal teacher ought to act. This ideal might include aspects which went beyond the duties of the teacher; it is seen as good or fine and as something which he chooses to pursue. This process can be morally admirable, depending of course on the details of the ideal.

We may contrast with this ideal-forming the role-playing of the man of *mauvaise foi*.[1] The man who plays a role out of 'bad faith' does so not because he has chosen to pursue a particular ideal but because he thinks that there is no other way in which he can behave. Sartre seems to distinguish a more and a less extreme form of this 'bad faith'. In the less extreme form – which is the third kind of role-playing – the individual pretends that he is nothing except what *other people want him to be*. That is, he acts the part which people have assigned to him, he 'plays up to expectations' and sees himself as whatever it is that other people want him to be. This is what is sometimes called 'playing the teacher'; it involves such things as adopting a style of clothes, voice and manner which are *not* part of the teacher's duties but which he thinks of as

[1] Jean-Paul Sartre, *Being and Nothingness*, pp. 47ff., translated by Hazel E. Barnes (London, Methuen, University Paperbacks, 1969).

'suitable', 'typical', etc. He may manage to confine his 'playing the teacher' to the classroom. But often his role becomes the essence of his self-conception, so that he sees every area of his life from the point of view of a particular role and finds it difficult either to take on other roles or to act in ways alien to this personality-integrating role. He will thus act out his role even when it is inappropriate; for example, the headmaster who begins by taking the rights and duties of his post too seriously may finish by 'acting the head-master' with his own children or with adult friends. In so doing a person completely pigeonholes himself, and so loses a sense of himself as an individual; this, as we have seen, involves a measure of loss of respect for himself. This kind of role-playing can easily lead to the more extreme form of *mauvaise foi*, in which the role-player pretends to be a thing, which has no choice and is causally determined. This type of behaviour is the analogue with regard to oneself of the first kind of impersonal attitude to others, and shows a basic lack of respect for oneself as a person.

5 Persons as idiosyncratic selves

Since it is a basic fact that there are differences in the physical endowment and psychological dispositions of people, we are conscious in typical human relationships of *this* individual or *that* individual, rather than of 'a person'. Moreover, it is as an *individual* that we most often want to be treated, rather than more abstractly as a person. Nor is this desire necessarily met by the individualistic aspect of *respect* which we noted in Section 3. On the contrary, the thought that some saintly figure is giving exactly the same degree of individual concern to everyone else that he is to oneself can be somewhat dismaying. What we want – some would argue that we also need it – is that someone should take an interest in us as individuals which would *not* be shown to everyone else. This demand is for a relationship with the idiosyncratic self.

But what *is* the idiosyncratic self? Clearly it is impossible – indeed, *logically* impossible – to characterize it in general terms, because it will consist of those manifestations of the generic self which make a person this individual rather than that. It follows that there can be no one attitude which is the morally or logically appropriate correlative of all idiosyncratic selves. In fact there cannot, strictly speaking, be attitudes directed towards an idiosyncratic self as such; for if an attitude is based on a belief about the nature of its object, as we have argued hitherto, it logically must be towards a person seen as falling into some class. There are, however, what we may call quasi-attitudes – states of mind resembling attitudes to a greater or lesser extent – which do necessarily have as their object some idiosyncratic self or other. In order to bring out more clearly the considerations we have in mind in introducing and using the concept of the idiosyncratic self we shall consider some examples of these quasi-attitudes, and their place in a teacher–pupil situation.

Take first affection.[1] Let us define 'affection' as a desire for another's welfare and happiness *as a particular individual*. This desire is thus to be distinguished from respect for persons. For the latter motive prompts us to seek others' good in general, whereas we want to say that those who feel affection feel a concern for another which they do *not* feel for everyone. Of course the 'respectful' man also concerns himself with the individual, as we saw earlier. But this means that he sees each individual as making separate claims which may not only compete with the majority interest but also differ in content from those of other individuals, whereas the concern of affection is not for *each* individual, but for *this* individual rather than others.

Affection does not seem to have any necessary connexion with the particular character of him for whom it is felt. If asked to explain why we are fond of someone, we *may* mention characteristics in him which stimulate affection, but it makes equally good sense to give a historical explanation – 'I've known him for a long time', 'I looked after him when he was ill' – or a biological one, such as 'He's my brother, after all'. Affection is in this sense non-rational, and in this way it differs sharply from ordinary attitudes.

It is natural and common for teachers and pupils to come to feel

[1] There is a discussion of some of these attitudes in Elizabeth Telfer, 'Friendship', *Proceedings of the Aristotelian Society*, 1971.

affection for each other: because long contact tends in itself to breed it, because they often go through painful struggles together (which again tends to foster it) and (in the case of small children) because the situation tends to be like a mother–child situation and to call forth in the parties something resembling natural maternal or filial affection. Moreover, there seems no difficulty in associating affection with a role-situation; even the most tightly structured hierarchies of roles (such as those of the army) are compatible with mutual affection, as between officers and their batmen. We have here the possibility of a teacher–pupil relationship (in the attitude sense of 'relationship') which is personal in a new sense, meaning 'directed to the idiosyncratic self'. Should teachers and pupils try to have this kind of personal relationship with each other?

Taken one way, of course, this question does not make sense: affection cannot be produced at will. But we can sensibly ask the slightly different question: is affection between teacher and pupil a good or a bad thing? Some would argue that to have a special concern for some people which one does not have for others is contrary to respect for persons. This of course is an attack on any case of affection, not simply that between teacher and pupils, and it raises the whole question of the place of 'special affections' in the moral life. Without investigating this problem in detail, we can suggest that, within the sphere of teachers' and pupils' duties, affection can add extra motivation for doing what in any case ought to be done and thus far is a good thing. But undue affection, if felt for some and not others, can make teachers or pupils *partial* – for example, make them take special trouble with marking a particular pupil's essay or preparing a particular teacher's homework – and this is a danger, though an avoidable one.

Outside the sphere of teachers' and pupils' duties to each other different problems arise. Here affection would be manifested, not in the motive from which duties are performed, but in performing actions which might not be undertaken at all in the absence of the affection: for example, a teacher may take the children on outings, and they may bring him presents or do odd jobs for him. Here again the main problem seems to be partiality: it would be all right for a teacher to take Primary 5B to the circus, but many people would hold that it would be wrong to take only Smith and Jones from 5B, even if the teacher does have a special affection for them. This verdict might in its turn be disputed, on the grounds that impartiality is called for only in the discharge of duties, not in non-duty situations; so long as Smith and Jones keep it to themselves, so as not to hurt the others' feelings, all is well. Something here turns on the age of the children. Of course teachers may well see this kind of extra-curricular activity not as an expression of affection but as part of their duties as teachers, and hence as something to be distributed impartially. We shall consider this view later.

Affection is not the only quasi-attitude, personal in the idiosyncratic sense, which is logically possible and morally permissible within the teacher–pupil relationship. Consider the quasi-attitude of liking. Liking is more like standard attitudes than affection in that normally we should expect reasons rather than causes to be proffered in explanation of it. But at the same time it resembles affection, and differs from attitudes proper, in that it is necessarily felt for the idiosyncratic individual. Thus I might give, as my reasons for liking James, that he is witty and gentle. But at the same time I like him not merely as one example of a witty and gentle person, for whom another such might be substituted, but as an individual whose uniqueness defies complete classification. Liking seems to be a quasi-aesthetic attitude, roughly specifiable as 'finding a person to one's taste', and depends partly on such things as his physical appearance, mannerisms, voice and speech, and style of life; partly on his traits of character, moral and other. The relative importance of these features as a basis for liking obviously depends on the liker.

This account of liking tends to suggest that before we can like someone we have to tot up items in his nature and strike a balance between the attractive and the unattractive aspects of it. But in reality our reaction, like a reaction to a picture, is to a whole personality seen as a unified thing. This is why we often find it very difficult to say what it is we like about a person. Sometimes what we like is partly the way in which everything about the person seems to 'hang together' and be part of a unified style; sometimes we enjoy a contrast, for example that between a mild unassuming exterior and an iron determination. Of course, the fact that we like a personality as a unity or whole does not rule out the possibility that we may dislike some individual features intensely. But in such a case we characteristically feel that these features are not merely objectionable in themselves, but also somehow mar or intrude upon a whole that is otherwise pleasing; and this fact sharpens our vexation.

The sense of a bond, or the sense that we have something in common with another person, is another idiosyncratic attitude. It can be distinguished from liking, for people can be ill-at-ease with those whom they like, and say things such as 'I like him, but I can't seem to communicate with him' or 'We don't talk the same language' or 'We don't seem to have much in common'. The bond may be seen in terms of shared interests or enthusiasms or views, but it may also be a similar style of mind or way of thinking which makes for a high degree of empathy.

Both liking and the sense of a bond can and do often exist within the teacher–pupil relationship. They are perhaps more commonly found where the pupils are nearer in age to the teachers and have more in common with them. The same kinds of problem arise as with affection, since liking and sense of bond also prompt activities – notably activities shared through pleasure in each other's company – which may suggest partiality.

It should be noted that personal relationships of the kind under discussion, consisting of idiosyncratic quasi-attitudes within the teacher–pupil set-up, may be unfavourable as well as favourable. Teachers and pupils can hate, dislike and feel estranged from each other. This is clearly a bad state of affairs, to be altered if possible – though it is of course possible for duties to be carried out despite idiosyncratic ill-feeling, from sense of duty. Some would say, however, that such feeling is better than the absence of all idiosyncratic quasi-attitudes, good and bad. This view may stem from a failure to realize that respect for persons in its own way takes account of the individual, but it may also be a plea for spontaneity in human dealings.

So far in this section we have been considering those attitudes personal in the sense of idiosyncratic, which can exist between teacher and pupil within their role-relationship. But older pupils who want a more personal relationship with their teachers often have in mind rather more than this: they are looking for a personal relationship in the 'situation' sense, in other words for something akin to friendship. To see what this further demand involves, let us briefly consider the nature of friendship.[1]

Before we can speak of a pair or group as friends, they must in fairly strong measure possess the feelings towards each other which we have been discussing: affection, liking, sense of a bond. They must also act upon these feelings in the behaviour thought to be characteristic of friends: performing services for each other, and sharing activities, both those of which the main point is that they are expressions of friendship, such as eating together, talking and exchanging letters, and also those which the friends would perform individually apart from the friendship, such as hobbies, worship and work. But these two conditions, though necessary, are not sufficient. What is also required is some kind of commitment to each other, in terms of an acknowledgment (in practice if not verbally) that there is a 'set-up'. This might manifest itself, for example, in the *assumption* by the friends that they will do things together and can call on each other for help in need.

So defined, friendship is a strong bond, but the term is also often used in a lighter way for what we may call 'companionship', especially when qualified, as in 'drinking friends', 'golfing friends', 'friends at work', etc. The companionship relationship differs from friendship in lacking strong feelings of affection (though there may be some) and in having a rather narrowly confined basis for the sense of a bond. Thus companions will not expect more than casual services from each other, or assume they will share the whole range of pursuits. This distinction between friends in our strong sense and companions is obviously not a sharp one, but rather a question of degree.

Our claim, then, is that those who wish for a personal relationship between teachers and pupils, in the sense of a bond or situation, have in mind something like friendship or companionship. This wish may however take three different forms: that the teacher–pupil role-relationship be *replaced* by a relationship of friendship; that a friendship relation be or be part of the role-relationship; and that it should exist alongside the role-relationship.

[1] See Telfer, op. cit.

Let us consider each in turn. The first form can be dealt with fairly briefly, in terms of our earlier discussion of the role-relationship of the teacher. The kind of situation sought by those who advocate the replacement view is exemplified by the Platonic picture of Socrates and his friends discussing philosophy. Now it may well be that Plato's account of Socrates' teaching provides the highest example we have of corporate intellectual endeavour, and that people should seek opportunities in their own way to follow this example. But it does not follow either that a given teacher and pupils can change their relationship into one of friendship, or that they should do so. Friendship cannot be forced; if a group do not have the relevant feelings for each other, friendship is impossible. Even where they do, however, or where there are the more restricted feelings involved in companionship, the maintenance of the role-relationship is imposed on them by their duties in respect of it to those outside the circle: the teacher to his employers, the pupils to the source of their livelihood, viz. parent or taxpayer. This is not to say that friendship may not grow up as it were *alongside* the role-relationship; we shall discuss this possibility later.

The second form of the demand for a personal relationship is that friendship should be part of the role-relationship. Now this idea does not make sense as it stands. A role-relationship consists simply of a set of rights and duties, whereas friendship, although it carries with it certain rights and duties, involves also the existence of certain attitudes, the characteristic behaviour to which such attitudes prompt one and the acknowledgment of the relationship. What does make sense, however, is the somewhat different idea that some of the *behaviour* characteristic of friends is among the accessory duties of the teacher's role. The practice of friendlike behaviour is what is normally referred to as 'being friendly to', as opposed to 'being a friend of', which refers to the fully-fledged friendship relationship.

Now it does seem to be the case that teachers are often held to have an accessory duty to behave in ways which can be described as being friendly to their pupils. Note that since this behaviour is now conceived of as a teaching *duty*, it is not idiosyncratic in the way friendship proper – as demanded on the replacement view –

is supposed to be: it has to be shown to all pupils *qua* pupils and not, like friendship, bestowed on one individual rather than another. Let us consider what friendly behaviour consists in, in the teaching context, and why it might be thought to be an accessory duty of teachers.

The behaviour characteristic of friends which was mentioned earlier fell into three categories: performing services, sharing cultural and other activities, and sharing social intercourse. All these things are in some measure expected of teachers. The services will typically be such things as lending books and equipment, recommending or defending pupils to outside bodies, and giving advice – not only when asked for but also when not asked for but needed. Extra-mural activities might include climbing expeditions or holidays abroad. Social occasions include the entertainment by teachers of pupils. (It is of course difficult to draw a sharp line between these categories.) Note that all these types of behaviour are not regarded as demanded to an unlimited extent. The teacher who lends books is doing his duty, the teacher who lends a car is heroic or misguided. Similarly, the teacher who takes children camping now and again may be performing a duty, but the teacher who never has a holiday except with pupils is going too far.

But more important than these specific types of behaviour is the employment, in carrying out both determining and accessory duties, of a general friendly *manner*. There are three elements in such a manner. Firstly, it is warm, receptive and encouraging, rather than cool and apparently detached. Secondly, it involves the teacher's revelation of himself as an individual: for example, by being enthusiastic about his own interests, being prepared to talk a little about his pursuits outside the teaching context, not disguising the fact that he has a domestic background, not putting on a mask to his pupils and above all showing a personal point of view towards the subject which is being taught, in the sense of conveying an awareness of its place in a total way of life. Thirdly, a friendly manner involves showing an awareness of the pupils as individuals, for example by taking an interest in their extracurricular pursuits and domestic backgrounds and by encouraging spontaneity from them.

There are two types of reason for regarding friendly behaviour of the kinds we have described as an accessory duty of the teacher. Firstly, it is conducive to the successful performance of his determining duties: pupils will normally learn more readily from someone who shows an interest in them and who can be seen as a rounded individual himself. Secondly, it is demanded by the general principle of respect for persons. This principle requires that we help others in the pursuit of goals and the achievement of standards. How we should fulfil this duty depends on our particular circumstances; but the teacher is as a rule particularly well-placed to serve his pupils in this way, not *qua* teacher, but *qua* adult who sees a lot of a group of young people, who may have a good deal of influence on them, and who may well be more leisured, wealthy and cultured than their parents. In helping pupils in this way, however, the teacher is clearly going beyond the duties of the teacher as such. The special factors on which these duties are based are connected only contingently with his position as a teacher, and indeed they do not always obtain.

It follows from this last point that the degree to which particular teachers are morally obliged to be friendly to their pupils depends on their individual circumstances. We said that the teachers may well be more leisured, more wealthy and more cultured than the pupils' parents. But this is not always so, and even where it is so they still may not be *sufficiently* well-endowed in these ways to be able to take on very much over and above their determining duties. For example, not all teachers have the facilities or the finances for entertaining on the scale which may be required; or they may have domestic commitments which do not give them the time for extensive activities with their pupils outside school hours. Again, a teacher may be interesting when discussing his subject and a complete bore otherwise. Students are mistaken in thinking that exclusion from staff common rooms cuts them off from stimulating intellectual conversation. Similarly in school teaching, there are few Jean Brodies[1] around, for good or ill.

But the most important limitations on a teacher's capacity to show friendly behaviour are those not of circumstances but of

[1] Muriel Spark, *The Prime of Miss Jean Brodie* (London, Macmillan, 1961).

character. For example, a teacher may be naturally a somewhat cold unsympathetic person who cannot adopt a genuinely friendly manner. It is true that sympathy can be cultivated to some extent, and also that the manner can to some extent be assumed. But there are limits to what is possible in this direction in the specially testing situation of the classroom, and also to the degree to which insincerity even where possible is permissible. In an extreme case we might want to say that the 'cold' teacher is in the wrong job. But there is room for the less extreme cases, especially with older pupils; the surly but sincere and conscientious teacher is often a respected figure. Again, a teacher may be *insufficiently* detached, and overwhelm his pupils with purposes which they do not really share, standards which they cannot yet evaluate for themselves, and an obtrusion of the details of his private life which amounts to an attempt to force an unwanted intimacy on them. This is the defect of the Jean Brodies, and it constitutes a failure in respect just as much as the lack of sympathetic warmth of the 'cold' teacher.

The third form of the demand for a personal relationship was that friendship should exist *alongside* the role-relationship. Now it is clear that such friendships logically could not be demanded as a duty from the parties concerned, since friendship, as distinct from the friendly behaviour we have just been discussing, is not something that can be produced to order. But it would make sense to suggest that such friendships should be regarded as a good thing, to be encouraged rather than inhibited where the possibility exists, and this is what pupils and teachers sometimes advocate.

Against this view, however, it may be argued that it is impossible for teachers and pupils to form friendships, in virtue of their continuing role-relationship (which cannot, as we saw earlier, be *replaced* by the friendship). This claim can take two forms: a psychological form, that it is as a matter of fact psychologically impossible for teachers and pupils to form friendships; and a logical form, that such an idea would not even make sense. We shall discuss the logical form first, as, if the claim can be upheld in that form, the psychological claim becomes irrelevant.

In what way might it be argued that it does not make sense

to speak of friendship between teacher and pupil? One possible argument is that it does not make sense to speak of friendship with someone with whom one has a role-relationship. Now as far as role-relationships in general go, this is clearly false. A man's doctor or his bank manager may be said to be a friend of his. The claim must therefore be that there is something about this particular role that is thought to be logically incompatible with friendship: for example, the fact that the teacher has a duty to try to get the pupil to do things (for his own good) which he may not want to do. But this is not a convincing argument against the possibility of teacher–pupil friendship. For one thing, it applies equally to the bank manager whose client has an overdraft or doctor whose patient has a weight problem, without our wanting to say that such pairs cannot be friends. In any case, friends in general often see themselves as having precisely such duties of interference for the other's good, in virtue of the friendship and quite apart from any other relationship which obtains between them.

It might however be argued that the teacher has, in virtue of his role, duties to outside bodies the performance of which may be unpleasant to the pupil; these duties, it might be thought, are incompatible with the duty of friendship to defend one's friend against others. But the latter duty, which we may call that of loyalty, is in any case by no means absolute. We can illustrate its limitations by referring again to the doctor and bank manager. The doctor has a duty to report his patient's notifiable disease to the Public Health Department, and the bank manager has a duty to give a true account of his client's bank interest to the Inland Revenue; these facts do not make us say that doctors and patients, or bank managers and clients, cannot be friends. Similarly, the fact that a teacher has a duty, say, to make reports on pupils (adverse if need be) to their parents or grant-paying bodies need not militate against the possibility of friendship between teacher and pupil. Indeed if the possession of a role entailing duties which might conflict with a friend's interests made friendship impossible, then there could be no such thing as friendship. For we all possess the role and the duties of a citizen, which might give rise to the duty to report a friend's crimes to the police.

But there remains an important consideration which distinguishes the teacher–pupil relationship from that between doctor and patient or bank manager and client, and which constitutes the real difficulty in the notion of friendship between teacher and pupil: the teacher is in a position of authority over the pupil and has a right to be obeyed. This essential inequality in their positions does seem to be a bar to friendship: not in the psychological sense, but in the sense that it seems difficult to apply the name of friendship to an unequal relationship.

There are two ways in which those eager to defend the possibility of teacher–pupil friendship might attempt to meet this argument: by showing that the teacher's authority leaves room for the equality required by friendship, and by denying that friendship requires equality. In pursuing the first of these lines, they will rightly point out that the teacher's authority is not all-embracing: he has a right to obedience within his sphere of competence, but not in any other aspect of life. It might seem therefore that a teacher and pupil could be friends out of school, as it were, where they can meet on terms of equality, and suspend the relationship within school, where the pupil is necessarily a subordinate. But this is a very difficult idea, not because such compartmentalizing is psychologically difficult, but rather because we defined friendship, as distinct from companionship, as a *pervasive* relationship which prompts the parties to it to share everything. Because of this, we should see relationships which exist out of but not in school as companionships. The question which remains about these is a psychological one: is it possible to suspend relationships in this way? Note that this will entail not only suspension of the companionship in school but also suspension of the teacher–pupil relationship outside it. We shall not discuss this question, which is really an empirical one, but simply point out that, whereas for many people it seems not only possible but easy, others who are busy 'playing the part of the teacher' find it very difficult.

The other possibility is to deny that friendship requires complete equality. This would have seemed nonsense to Aristotle, who thought of equality as a necessary condition for true friendship and hence denied that proper friendship was possible between master and slave or even between husband and wife.[1] But in fact it is not clear why one should insist on complete equality for friendship. It might be said that inequality prevents the existence of the sense of a bond, which we made a necessary condition of friendship. But whether or not it does this surely depends on how the parties view the inequality. If one rejoices in it while the other chafes against it, or if one acknowledges it while the other does not – as might happen in Aristotle's cases – then perhaps there is a difference between them which is too major for the sense of a bond to exist. This is the kind of situation where people sometimes say, 'If *that*'s how he looks at this important issue, we simply don't talk the same language'; and whereas this can be said of any major difference, for example about politics or religion, it makes even better sense where the difference is one that will necessarily colour the whole relationship, as in the cases where it concerns the status of the parties relative to each other.

If on the other hand both parties are agreed that there are spheres in which one has the authority, and agreed on the reasons which justify this authority, the inequality, far from preventing a bond, might be an added bond. In the teacher and pupil case the justification for the authority depends on the nature of the end which they presumably share: if they love learning and the pursuit of truth, they will both acquiesce happily in the degree of authority which is a necessary means to the achievement of their shared purpose, because he who wills the end also wills the means. Where this is the case, why should we not say that recognition of the necessary authority is a possible element in the bond?

We suggest then that there is no logical impossibility in the idea of friendship between teacher and pupil. The difficulties are rather psychological ones: for example, even where the requisite quasi-attitudes exist (and we must stress again that these cannot be forced) there are the difficulties which arise if the inequality which is appropriate in certain spheres is allowed to extend beyond its due place. The cure for this tendency is presumably the steadfast recognition by each party that he himself and his friend are individuals – the refusal to pigeonhole himself or the other. If this is

[1] Aristotle, *Nicomachean Ethics*, 1158b1 seq., 1161b1. But cf. 1161a20, 1162a16.

possible – and it seems implausible to assume it is not – then we may say that teacher and pupil can be friends.

It remains to consider very briefly what is to be said about the pros and cons of such friendship. The dangers and drawbacks are, as before, those of actual partiality, together with the possibility that the teacher will be *thought* partial and so forfeit the confidence of other pupils. But if these dangers can be avoided – and how far this is possible depends very much on the particular circumstances – then the benefits are great; not only because such a friendship is instrumental to education but also because friendship is in itself a rare and worthwhile thing, to be sought and cultivated for its own sake wherever it can be found.

6 Conclusion

In this chapter we have discussed the nature of the relationships (in the 'attitude' sense of that word) which may obtain between teacher and pupil. We began by pointing out that the attitudes teacher and pupil may have to each other can be divided into three types according to whether they were directed to the other person simply as a person, as a member of a class or group or as a particular individual. These types, however, are all to be contrasted with the objective type of attitude which treats a person as a causally determined thing. We suggested that the teacher's attitude to his pupil should be reactive rather than objective: that is, it should recognize his pupil's nature as a person. It should also incorporate respect for persons; in other words, it should show due regard for the various aspects of the characteristic human endowment. We then turned to the attitudes directed towards people as members of a group, and came to the conclusion that there was nothing impersonal, in an untoward sense, in the categorizing involved in forming such attitudes. But 'pigeonholing', or regarding a person (oneself or another) solely in terms of some category, was shown to be contrary to respect for persons. Finally we discussed attitudes, or rather quasi-attitudes, to people as individuals, and their place within a teacher–pupil context; also the question how far the notion of friendship between teacher and pupil makes sense. On this last question we concluded that, whereas friendship cannot replace the role-relationship or form part of it, it can logically exist alongside it; and that, though such friendships obviously have their dangers, they can also be valuable.

Postscript

We have presented portions of this book as papers to various philosophy of education societies and have found that certain types of objection are often levelled at our arguments. Although some of them have already made their appearance and have been discussed in specific contexts in the body of the book, we should like to deal with them systematically at this point.

The most common is that our conception of education or of the teacher is much too narrow. Our reply is that there are gains in clarity resulting from a narrow conception of a teacher and of an educated man, for it thereby becomes more possible to contrast the wise man or the good man or the cultured man with the educated man and to see what they have in common and how they might differ. The narrow view is based on certain traditional conceptions of education and of the teacher, although of course our description of the educated man has a large element of stipulation in it. Our narrow conception, however, is only *conceptually* normative. In adopting this conception, that is, we are recommending only that educatedness be seen in a certain way and not that it be preferred to other end-states; our separate discussion, about the possibility of justifying the pursuit of education in our sense, suggested fairly modest conclusions on the value of education. The fact that our narrow conception of education is only conceptually normative enables us to adopt a second line of defence against those who object to it: that if it seems to some to be preferable to use 'education' in a broad sense, and to say that whatever the teacher does in school he is doing *qua* teacher, our analysis can then be regarded as distinguishing different components within this broad conception.

A second objection is that our view of education is élitist. This term is now much in use as a term of abuse, but its meaning is not always clear. In an educational context three meanings can perhaps be distinguished, which we shall mention in turn. Firstly, the charge may be that our view of education favours an economic élite with a secure financial position, in that the emphasis has been put on traditional subjects as distinct from those useful in earning a living. The initial reply to this is to repeat that the narrow sense of education we have been advocating is intended to be only conceptually normative. We are not saying that pupils should spend their time or governments their money on education in our sense; it might well be better all round if more money were spent on vocational studies. Our point is simply to query whether it is helpful to regard these as part of education. But having said this, we can go on to ask whether it is not our opponents who are guilty of élitism here; their objection seems to be based on an assumption that the majority have no interest or welfare beyond earning a living and that cultivation of the mind concerns only the few.

The second meaning of the charge of élitism is that we cater for an élite in terms of ability, since not everyone is able to pursue education in our sense. That not everyone is intellectually capable of the highest reaches of education in our sense is certainly true, but to say this is quite compatible with saying that young people should be given the opportunity of pursuing education as far as they can. In any case, we would maintain that almost everyone is capable of acquiring some degree of what we have called educatedness. Again, one wonders whether it is not the objector who is in a sense élitist in underrating the capacities of the ordinary person.

The third type of charge of élitism is more complex than the others: it is that the very content of what we have called educatedness is somehow middle-class, and ignores 'working-class culture'. Several different things may be meant here. One possible meaning is that teachers often endeavour to inculcate 'posh' accents and table-manners alien to the children's background; these attempts

are not, however, part of *education* as we have describ
serving some complementary aim. But sometimes c
seen as middle-class in some sense. This may simply
that the middle class has taken more interest in it.
is supposed to be that there are working-class cultural figure
movements which are wrongly neglected by us in favour of a so-
called middle-class culture, then our reply would be that the cultural heritage is what it is for reasons unconnected with class:
if a claim can be sustained, on aesthetic grounds, that the Beatles'
songs are worthwhile as songs, then they could and should pass
into the canon.

The third main objection to our point of view is that it is *re-actionary*. But this objection is mistake on two levels. Firstly, it
assumes that we are recommending, as distinct from analyzing, our
admittedly traditional conception of education. But secondly, it
assumes that we see old-fashioned schooling as the way to produce the educated man in our sense. This, however, is far from
the case; it may well be that modern educational methods will produce something nearer to what we have called the educated person
than traditional methods usually did.

A fourth objection is that our narrow conception of education
is too rationalistic: we stress 'the mind' at the expense of 'the
emotions'. It must be remembered, however, that we do make room
for the appreciation of art, etc. in our conception of education.
Moreover, it may be that those who level this kind of objection
are operating with a dualistic view of the mind and the emotions
which we would reject. To educate the mind in the ways we have
suggested is *ipso facto* to educate the emotions. Those who are
seeking something more are probably seeking not educatedness but
culture, or perhaps the raw experience of life itself. Nothing we
say must be taken to suggest that these things are not valuable; our
theme is just that they are different from educatedness.

The final objection we shall consider is the most fundamental one:
what, it may be asked, is the use of all this theorizing? What we need
in education is empirical research about the most effective methods,
not philosophical analysis. The answer to this kind of objection
is threefold. Firstly, we can point to the practical applications

suggested in the preface: our discussion will, we hope, help to clarify thought about education at a time when there is a great deal of public debate about it. Secondly, we can point out that empirical research, while obviously vital, is about means and not ends. Moreover, it presupposes a notion of what the aim is: one cannot find out the best way to do something without having a clear idea of what that something is. Consideration of the teacher's aims, therefore, is as essential for the educational psychologist as for the teacher himself, and we hope to suggest one possible way in which his aims may be regarded. Thirdly, we suggest that an activity need not have a use in order to have a point or value; as we said in our essay, the exercise of the theoretical reason, exemplified in writing philosophy, may be regarded as good in itself.

Index